Too often history has been told by kings and those with power. But sometimes, just sometimes, there is a moment when a group of ordinary men somehow manage to change the world. The names of these heroes have been hidden away, until now. Its time the tale were told, of Harry, Vic Flange, Derryck Trotter, Arthur Day, Pieshop, Rigalaroni Tony, and Icky Custard.

WE APPY FEW

By

Alex Duggan.

Also, by Alex Duggan

Non-fiction -

WHO KILLED THE ESSEX BOYS

JONBENET RAMSEY, THE GREAT AMERICAN TRAGEDY

WHO KILLED STEPEHN WARD

JACK THE RIPPER, INTO THE DARKNESS

Fiction -

HATFUL OF HOLLOW

HOLIDAYS IN THE SUN

Copyright ©Alex Duggan 2025

Happiness, something in my own place
I'm stood here naked, I smile and I feel no disgrace
With who I am
Happiness, coming and going
I watch you look at me, watch my fever grow
And I know just who I am
      THE VERVE

PART ONE

ENGLAND, MY ENGLAND

8

Chapter 1

If history were taught in the form of stories, it would never be forgotten.
    Rudyard Kipling

London. 23rd October 1501 AD (After Dinner)

You want to know what happened, very well, I shall tell you. But I am over one hundred years old. My memory plays tricks on me. I have been here before. When I was a boy. The same tapestries on the walls, the same bars on the windows looking out at the Tower of London.

I have not met King Henry before. That would be King Henry the seventh. Of his two sons, Arthur, the heir apparent, seems a sallow spotty youth devoid of any personality, like a postulant frog. The young Henry, not even ten, acts bullish. Perhaps he senses he will never be king, or will always be ginger. I understand representatives from the Spanish royal family are here to oversee the marriage between the thirteen-year-old Arthur and the fourteen-year-old Catherine of Aragon. They have brought with them a black servant, John Blanke. I know one man who would have called that "The Eternal Recurrence."

Near a window sits a man behind a long narrow desk. He waits with a quill in his hands. Nearby is a pile of paper, and a jar of ink. Behind him is Sir Andrew Marl, a beak like mean spirited pontificator who comes forward to start formal proceedings.

'You are Harold Thatcher, *alleged* to be over a hundred years old?'
'No,' I reply.

This brings the room to a sudden hush. My face has more wrinkles than my grey-haired scrotum, but these lines are due to being a hundred years old rather than a cocksure charlatan. 'I find the use of the word "alleged" to be political rather than biological. Could you kindly refrain from using such language.' I may have been born a poor cockney with nothing but holes in my pockets, but I was certainly born over a hundred years ago.

Sir Andrew Marl is clearly not used to being spoken to in this manner. He rubs the skin under his chin. I wait for this pompous rantallion to regain his composure.

'But you are Harold Thatcher?'

Again, I decide not to give a subservient reply. Any concession now will lead to me having to call him 'sir.' I look at the young prince.

'Call me Harry.'

Sir Marl spoke again, continuing to address the audience rather than myself. 'You are *believed* to be the last surviving person to have been at the Battle of Agincourt?' He spoke as if I was on trial for heresy.

I smile. 'I will be guided by your *certainty* that you have checked with the rest of the world as to that remark; all I can say is that I was there.'

Sir Marl grunts slightly. 'The King wants you to give an account of those events. Are you able to do that?'

'Very well,' I reply. 'If you want to know what happened, I shall tell you.' I wait for the man to dip his quill. 'But do you want the truth, or do you want a good story?'

The gasps are louder this time. The King is second only to God. I look over at the maid for Catherine of Aragon. She blushes. She probably thinks I am a dirty old man. She is right. I've always had a thing for wenches' uniforms. Prince Henry spares the room any further embarrassment.

'Both,' he says. 'I want to hear how Henry the Fifth saved England and I want to hear all about the battle.'

The King raises his hand.

'Agincourt was in 1415. How are you able to tell the difference between the truth and a story when it come to the past?'

'Your majesty,' I reply. 'I am limited by my language and time. Henry the Fifth did win the Battle of Agincourt, that is history. What happened to me is a story.' I look at an old tapestry of three lions that dominates the wall behind the King. 'If I may, I shall start from the beginning, as it will help me recall certain events.'

The King nods. I wait for the man to dip his quill again. 'Now, if you want to know what happened, very well, I shall tell you.'

Chapter 2

Do you know what nemesis means?
    Bricktop, Snatch.

London. June 1415

My father was a steeplejack. He would tie a rope around me, and we would climb up the highest churches to look down on a London that very few people had seen. He would point out how even the most important people looked small from here and that I could be anything I wanted if I aimed high enough. The job was extremely dangerous, but it had its rewards. As payment, the monks at All Hallows taught me how to read and write.

In 1413 my father was given work in the Tower of London. I was thirteen years old and had never seen so many wonderous sights. The clothes, carriages, boats, animals, were all things I had only read about until now. The only sad thing was I knew I did not want to be a steeplejack. Books had placed the world in my mind and I wanted to see it for real.

One day we were approached by the royal menagerie keeper, Sir Jeffrey Bernard. He wanted me to help treat the King's elephant. I went past three cages by the river Thames which held the lions. In the last cage was my first elephant. Sir Jeffrey explained that beast had scratches on its back, but no one could get on top of it to heal the wounds. In truth two men had tried and fallen, one seriously injured. The simple solution was it was that a boy should do it. My father insisted that if it worked, I was to be taken on as an apprentice. After much consternation,

Sir Jeffrey agreed. He expected me to be killed by the afternoon anyway.

My father took me to one side and said this would be my chance to have a better life than him. He didn't want me to spend the rest of my life in a dead-end job. He was right in other ways as well, for within the year, he would be dead. I made the decision to ride the elephant.

Sir Jeffrey was surprised when I asked if I could read manuscripts about the creature first. We went off to the royal library. I never realised how beautiful so many books together looked. My Latin was better than my Greek. I found out the elephant was from a place called Africa, ate mainly vegetation, and that the long proboscis was rather like a nose that could be used as an arm. Both male and female elephants had tusks made of ivory. I blushed slightly when I read that the male elephant has a six-foot penis and testicles twice the size of a human head.

Then I found a book about an ancient general called Hanibal, who used elephants in his army. As they crossed the Alps, some of the elephants were injured. Hannibal would clean the wounds with wine, use a mixture of mint and honey as a compote, then a cover of dock leaves, finally tying a rug over the scratches until they had healed. Sir Jeffrey was impressed and agreed to try it. That was the easy part.

The lions in the next cages roared as the magnificent elephant was brought out to the courtyard. It took a while for me to comprehend just how large this creature was. The sound of it pissing onto flat stone was like a thousand hooves drowning my ears. I took a step back and dried my face. I explained that Hanibal used bread dipped in wine to placate the elephants first. Sir Jeffrey took a bottle while I put three loaves into a bucket of wine. I let the elephant take it with its trunk. Having never drunk wine myself, I had no idea what effects it would have on the creature. The elephant seemed to enjoy it. I let the creature take some more bread as I climbed up onto the back of the elephant.

I poured wine over the scratches. Some of them were quite deep. I quickly smothered warm mint and honey over the wounds. Dock leaves soaked in wine were put into place. Lastly, I rolled a rug over the elephants back. Once down, I gave the elephant the last loaf while Sir Jeffrey tied the rug. The elephant was rewarded with the bucket of wine while Sir Jeffrey rewarded himself by finishing the bottle.

The elephant walked over to a stone archway, leaned against it, took another long steaming piss, then promptly fell asleep. I went over to check. The elephant used an old postern as a scratching post. It had worn away the ancient stone until a Roman nail was sticking out. I climbed on the elephant. It released such a tremendous fart that I wondered if the building would survive. I pulled the nail out. When I came down, a tall man with a scar on his face approached me.

'I see the farty old beast is drunk again,' he said, waving his hand in front of his face.

'I got the idea from Hannibal,' I replied. 'It was the only way I could treat the elephant.'

The tall man thumbed towards a drunken vet urinating against the wall. 'I was talking about Sir Jeffrey. What was wrong with the elephant?'

I showed him. The tall man took the nail and walked away.

From then on, Sir Jeffrey Bernard not only made me his apprentice, he allowed me to borrow books from the royal library. And now two years later I had gained an education that only the very rich could have. Of course, having no title or land, I was still clearing out elephant shit, but at least I had learnt the Latin name for it.

Now we come to 1415. I was fifteen years old and sorting out the elephant after it had eaten three bushels of ripe plums. Every time it farted it would fire out the large fruity seeds with a big "whump." By lunchtime it had already killed two ravens. Sir Jeffrey said he was unwell after a bad lamb chop and had gone to lie down with a nice bottle of Chianti. I was left to feed the lions.

In the courtyard that day were a group of noblemen showing off to a coterie of young maidens. I confess that the sight of these pretty women stirred something in me, and my concentration lapsed. Somehow, the door to the middle cage was opened and a lion escaped. A damsel in distress screamed. I ran up with my wooden shovel, thinking she had stepped in something nasty. The lion growled at me. I pretty much did something nasty in my trousers.

The lion followed me until I came to the open cage door. I took my key out of the lock and stepped inside. Probably the most stupid thing I could have done. At this point I realised that I was trapped. The lion decided that I was an easier meal. It hunched its back as it moved into the cage. And then it stopped. I waited. The lion knew it had all the time in the world. What saved me was a plum I had in my pocket. From the corner I threw it to the other corner. The lion watched it roll on the ground. He took a sniff and stepped forward. There was hardly any space. I moved around as the beast wondered which food to go for, and I smacked the lion on the arse with the shovel. It jumped forward as I jumped out of the cage. My hand was shaking so much I struggled to turn the lock. The lion looked at me as I heard the girls cheering. I smiled. Someone slapped me on the side of my head.

'You, excrement breath. You put these poor maidens life in danger.'
I held on to the key. 'No, I never.'
The man wore an outfit of red and gold frills, with an enormous, studded codpiece. He slapped me again. 'You

impudent little turd. How dare you. If it wasn't for me bravely calling out from on top of that wall, you could have killed this lady I just saved.' He put his hands on his hips and parted his legs. 'Do you know who I am?'

'The court jester?'

He slapped me a third time. 'I am Lord Farquar. Who are you?' He did not wait for an answer. 'Who are you?'

Sir Jeffrey Bernard ran over and explained that it couldn't have possibly been me who had a hand in leaving the lions cage door open, as my arm was in an elephant's anus at the time. But Norman Farquar refused to listen and demanded justice. Sir Bernard told me to go back to the storehouse to wash my hands while he tried to find out what had happened.

I was still cursing this idiot when two guards appeared with orders to take me to the white tower. This was bad news. Even if no one could prove I opened the lions cage, I had let the keys out of my sight, which was still a punishable offence. The privy council were more likely to believe the word of a lairy Lord than a cockney reject. I walked across the courtyard, wondering if I should just make a run for it. I barely noticed all the activity going on around me. Riders came over the cobbles carrying the banners of the royal messengers, their horses covered in sweat.

I was marched up the stone steps and taken to the Great Room. A group of men were watching a large tapestry of three heraldic lions being hung onto the wall. Farquar and Sir Jeffrey were waiting with the tall man I had met before. He turned. It was King Henry the Fifth. He bade me over.

'First Hannibal and now Samson. You appear to be made out of history books. I hear you fought a lion today?'

I was about to agree when I saw Lord Farquar standing nearby. I shook my head. 'The lion fought itself, and lost,' I replied, then adding, 'Your Majesty.'

The King seemed interested in my answer. 'Explain?'

'The lion believed it was bigger and more powerful than me, and so it fell easier into the trap.'

King Henry stood over six foot tall and had a scar on his face. He also had a fearsome reputation. He looked closely at me. 'Who are you?'

'My father fought alongside you at the Battle of Shrewsbury,' I replied. He was standing close enough to see you hit by an arrow.'

'Who is your father?'

Before I could tell him that my father had drowned in the docks, a messenger came in.

'News from France, your majesty.'

The King focused on the messenger. 'What is the French Kings reply?'

'Balls, your majesty.' The messenger held up two tennis balls. 'King Charles gave us no instructions, but the Dauphin of Paris wished to pass on this message.' The messenger handed over the tennis balls.

King Henry knew what they meant. That he was too young to be involved in matters of state and would be better off playing games. The people waited to hear his reply. The King turned and threw a ball at a tapestry on the wall. 'He has taken over our land in France, and now he thinks he can invade us at any time. He must be stopped.'

Others began to whisper amongst each other. I was guided back to the door by Sir Jeffrey.

'Don't worry. I've dealt with people like this little Farquar before.'

As we reached the archway another voice called out.

'Your majesty. What of the peasant's punishment?' Lord Farquar pointed at me. 'A rich lady almost died because of his mistake.'

The King looked at me. 'I give you a choice. Stand trial against your accuser, or volunteer to defend your country.'
Defending my country from the rigours of a French invasion sounded better than being a defendant in a rigged trial 'I will do my bit for England, your majesty.' I didn't have a clue what he was talking about, but it sounded the easier option. I was led out of the room as the generals started making plans.

At the top of the stairs Farquar ran over and grabbed me by the shoulder.

'Trying to brown nose the King were you boy? That's my job. I am going to make your life such a living hell that you will wish for the French to put you out of your misery.' He slapped me again, knowing if I showed any sign of retaliation I would surely be put into jail. It was only his desire to get back into the room that he did not push me down the stairs.

Back in his office, Sir Jeffrey finished his wine and slowly shook his head.

'You stupid boy. It's not England the King wants you to defend, it's the English owned land in France that's up for grabs. He is going to build an army to go over there to get that land back.'
There was hope. He explained to me that an army is made up of many units. Some a lot easier than others. With my knowledge of anatomy, he would write a letter for me to be given work as an apprentice in the physician's unit. I would be looking after wounded Knights far away from any battle. Sir Jeffrey then stopped. He had seen me practice my archery in the courtyard. I was very good. He would often bet against the Kings archers in a shooting match, where I would deliberately miss until the stakes were raised, and then I would hit the bullseye. Sir Jeffrey asked if I wanted to join the Kings bowmen or stay well away from danger? I looked at my father's longbow leaning against the wall. Next to it the large wooden shovel with my name on

it. Did I want to spend the rest of my life in a cage covered in elephant shit or spend one day as a lion before getting killed. For the second time that day I took the easier option and requested the letter.

As a leaving gift, Sir Jeffrey showed me a clasp of polished ivory from an elephant's tusk. He slid it down the top of the longbow until it stuck tight. It would be like my own banner. People would ask questions about it, and I could reply by telling them I was an apprentice at the tower.

As I looked at the six -foot long Yewtree bow what had once belonged to my father. It was only in the last year that I had been strong enough to use it. I was not ready for change, but change was coming whether I wanted it to or not. Looking back at this moment I had no idea what the future held for me.

Chapter 3

This happy breed of men.
  William Shakespeare.

The whole of London was talking about King Henry raising an army to fight the French. knights from every shire were willing to serve just show their banners in battle. Foot soldiers would be paid well and given new armour. The longbow archers would be paid a few shillings a day. The last group would be made up of cooks, knights' servants, physicians servants, tent and arrow makers, cooks, and numerous other helpers. They would still have to be able to fire an arrow or hold a sword. They would be the lowest paid but had more chance of coming back.

I walked through the busy narrow streets of the east end with a letter from my master in my pocket and my father's longbow at my side. A proper wide boy. The law was that you were not allowed to have the bow stringed in public, but a better-quality bow always got a bit of attention. Mine was freshly waxed and had a bit of ivory on it.

The town criers were calling for men to meet at Hackney Marshes to prove their archery skills and join up. I needed to speak to my mum first. She worked in one of the bakers in Pudding Lane and had done since my father had died. My elder sister was married off, and it was her father-in-law, Edwin Farriner, who owned the shop. I knew my mother would only let me leave if I gave my younger brother the apprenticeship at the tower. If I told her that I had been accused of something I had not done, she would have made me stand up and swear on the Bible I was innocent. But as my dad had committed suicide, his sin would become public knowledge. I didn't want that grief for my mum all over again. As a treat I carried home some bones from the lion's cage so that she could make soup with them.

I would tell my mother that I wanted to go, that my father had fought for this country, and I wanted too as well. I would also show her letter saying that I would be put in the physician's unit, keeping me far away from enemy lines. My mum couldn't read, but even she knew a good thing when she saw it.

'Just be careful when you go to Hackney Marshes,' she said. 'And tell them you can read and write; and tell them that the King's own animal doctor wants you to join the physician's unit.' She stirred the bones. 'And don't forget to go back to the tower to tell Sir Jeffrey that Richard can take over your apprenticeship while you're in France.'

For the first time I realised that I could be going over the sea.

'How long do you think it will last?'

'Who knows,' my mum replied, 'You should be back before Winter. Just make sure you get in with one of the physicians. You never see a poor doctor. All their mistakes get buried. And make sure you take a scarf.'

'Mum, its baking outside.'

'The sun might be different over there. That's why the French have so much facial hair.' She gave me a hug. 'You just stay safe, you hear me. Your dad would be proud of the young man you've become. You got an education and an apprenticeship, and now you're going off working for a doctor. He wanted you to take all the chances and to do all the things that he had never done.'

I had heard this story already, many times. 'Did he ever talk about the battle?'

She bent down and removed a small pouch from behind the stove. 'Just in case you need it.' She went to hand me a few pennies. I refused. She looked at the clasp on the top of my longbow.

'What's that?'

'Ivory, from an elephant's tusk. In Africa it proves you are a warrior.'

She took the longbow and turned it upside down. 'You see these small black marks here. Your father started marking the number of people he killed. He said he got to ten and then stopped.' She handed me back the longbow. 'Just remember, in the end it will be God who judges your actions and decides if you get in or not.' She hugged me as if it would be the last time, I would ever see her. I was only going up the road. She also slipped the coins into my pocket.

I went to Whitechapel market to buy some good arrows. The narrow streets were crowded with people either selling, buying, or stealing. Occasionally the noise would be interrupted when passing a local ale house, where music or swearing would join the chorus of prostitutes touting for business. Add to this the cries of animals waiting to be slaughtered, and you had the typical shopping experience of London.

I knew the arrow stall keeper's son, Rodney. We had been friends for years. I had never met anyone else who preened so much over their hair. He would wash it regularly once a month, even when it wasn't dirty. Rodney's family made good quality arrows; real goose feathers tied with silk. With the odd ones that couldn't be sold, we would sometimes go to the country to practice. I saw Rodney wearing a claret and blue tunic speaking to the man on the next stall. I tapped him on the shoulder.

'Gone a bit flash, innit.'

He pointed at the clasp on my longbow. 'look oo's talkin.'

'You'll never make a King's lookout,' I told him.

'No need bruv,' he replied, flicking the hair away from his face. 'They offered me the armoured regiment with the duke of

York. I get nearly twice as much as an archer, and a new pair of boots. Forget about carrying a longbow, join the foot regiment with me.'

I showed him the letter. 'I'm going to join the physician's unit, looking after the wounded knights.'

'But you'll miss all the fighting.' Rodney flicked his head back. I wondered how he would ever cope wearing a helmet. The guy behind him would have a nosebleed the first time they all stood to attention.

'I get to look after all these wounded rich knights who are always going to give a good tip. Plus, if they lose a hand, I will keep the jewellery. I'm going to make a killing by keeping them alive.'

Rodney brushed a hand through his hair. 'Think of the crumpet if we tell them we are front line soldiers. We can say we've killed a hundred French knights and saved England. They would stick to us like witch smoke. Anyway, when was the last time you missed the target? They will put you in an archery division even with that letter.'

I tapped the side of my nose. 'Don't worry, I have a cunning plan.'

After explaining my idea, discussing what we would do to the young wench working on the wimple stall, and choosing a few arrows, Rodney said his training would be in Colchester. Then down to Winchester, and hopefully onto France. His birthday came before mine, and now he was sixteen he could apply for extra duties.

'They've got these things called cannons,' he said. 'Six-foot-long pipes that fire big iron balls that can knock down castle walls.' It all sounded like an elephant's penis to me, but Rodney continued. 'The unit that moves and loads these cannons will get even more money. A right cushty number. By the time we get back home I would have earned enough to get a little business going.'

'Why don't you bring back three of those balls,' said the little market trader on the next stall. 'You could set up a pawn shop.' I told them that I could earn more money taking a knight's ring than handling a soldier's balls. At that moment a nun walked past. She shook her head and gave the sign of the cross. It was a message to get to the marshes to put Gods plan into action.

Chapter 4

Hi, Vivian Stanshall, trumpet
Big hello to big John Wayne, xylophone
And Robert Morley, guitar
Billy Butlin, spoons
And looking very relaxed, Adolf Hitler, on vibes. Nice!
Princess Anne on sousaphone
Introducing Liberace, clarinet.
  The Bonzo Dog Doo-Dah Band, The Intro and the Outro song.

Hackney Marshes was used by commoners for grazing livestock. Tt was big enough for archery clubs to practice and have competitions. Pub teams would meet up, have a bit of a flick about, then go and get pissed. Today there were thousands of men being herded around numerous pitches. Those who shot well were sent to one marquee to sign up for the archery units. Those who did badly were told to leave. The average would go to the various tents on the edge of the tree line. I went out and fired my first three arrows, all hitting the target, and all missing the bullseye. I was handed a small parchment marked with a red circle. Having passed the first test, I was directed towards another pitch.

In this tent I had a medical by someone who must have previously worked sexing piglets. When he asked me about my longbow, I gave the Latin name for my shoulder bones. He was not impressed.

'Do you think you're too good for the archery regiment, boy?' I shook my head. 'No sir. It's just that I can read and I want to work in the physician's unit.'

He gave me back my card. 'Go to pitch number six. But I warn you, miss the target just once, and you will be working in the field kitchen. At least you will be able to read the menu.'

I went to the next section. The heat seemed to rise from the ground. It would make the arrows lighter. The target was further away. With three decent arrows I hit the mark every time, but never a bullseye. A man checked my score and then told me I was not good enough for the archery regiment but was eligible to join a camp unit. I asked for the physician's tent. He pointed to the marquee that flew a green flag with a gold staff and snake.

The men inside seemed more interested in drinking the ale than healing the sick. I went up to a man sat writing into a ledger. He held up a magnifying glass and looked at me.

'How old are you?'

'Fifteen, sir. Nearly sixteen.'

'What's your archery score?'

'Thirty-six.'

He looked at me again, and then at my bow. 'Where did you get that from?

'It was my father's.'

'Don't fancy working for a knight, riding a horse. Most boys your age do.'

I shook my head. 'I already have an apprenticeship, at the tower, with Sir Jeffrey Bernard, looking after the royal menagerie. I have a letter requesting I be given a job in the physician's unit.' I searched my pockets, but the letter had gone.

'Not lying are you boy?' The man looked closely at me. 'Not trying to get out of doing your duty to your country because you are too frightened to fight?'

'No sir,' I replied. 'I can speak Latin, Greek and a bit of French. I know how to apply healing plants for certain ailments and how to treat wounds.'

'You've worked on injured soldiers?'

'No.'

He looked up at me. 'I suppose animal anatomy is similar to humans. What is the largest thing you've ever treated?'

'An elephant's penis.' This did not seem to go down well. 'I did have a letter from the tower, honestly sir.'

The man pointed to someone in the corner, 'Then I suppose you know that bloke over there who also had a letter from Sir Jeffrey Bernard.'

I turned. Holding a jug of ale and laughing with a group of other men was the market trader who had the stall next to Rodney. When he saw me, he came over and put his arm on my shoulder.

'Cor Blimey. Hello young Harry. It's your old mate Derryck' He turned to the man behind the desk. 'I can vouch for this boy, your worship. He is an absolute diamond. Having him on this unit will be like me not even being there.'

The man looked at him through a magnifying glass. 'And you can speak French as well?'

Jawohl,' Derryck replied.

The man wrote my name then turned the manuscript around to face me. 'Most people just put an X.'

I dipped the quill and wrote my full name.

'Look at that,' said Derryck. 'The number of times I've caught him playing with his nib.'

'What was he writing?' The man asked.

Derryck shrugged. 'I was speaking metaphorically, your honour.'

The man took back his ledger and looked at me. 'You will be in physician's unit number three. Your specific roles will be given to you later.' He gave me a coin. I was now officially a Kings subject.

Derryck took me by the arm and led me over to a group of men. I wanted to ask how he got the same letter but did not get time.

   'Lads, this is Harry Thatcher. He's joined our team.'
A man with a farmer's fringe and Liverpudlian accent looked at me. 'As what, the mascot?'
   'This is Icky Custard,' said Derryck. 'Don't worry about the haircut, it's a northern thing. He's a herbalist. Expert on Mushrooms.'
I could see that he had already taken a few.
   'Got a bird?' Icky asked. 'Or a sister?'
Derryck put his arm around my shoulder again. 'Ignore him. Just watch your wheels when you leave your cart outside overnight.' He then pointed to one of the largest men I have ever seen. 'This is Pieshop, he's…'

~

Back to the present -
Sir Andrew Marl stopped me.
   'Excuse me. I know this happened over eighty years ago, but your story includes a character called Pie Shoppe?'
 'This is not a story,' I replied. 'And he is not a character, he was my friend. For the record, he was called Pieshop, not Pie Shoppe.' I looked around. 'Perhaps all questions should be left until the end.'
Henry Tudor agreed, and nodded for me to continue.

~

Where was I. Oh yes, Derryck Hollins, a man who ducked and dived like a donkey's nob in a field of nettles, continued introducing me to the others.
   'This is Pieshop, he's a carpenter by trade.' The big, bearded man nodded. His longbow could have been cut from the same

Yew tree as my fathers. I wondered why he had not joined the Archery units. Built like a clay shithouse, he stared at me until my legs began to buckle.

Derryck moved me along and pointed at a tall man wearing a green hat. 'This is Vic Flange. From the west country. Plays the lute. Used to be a troubadour.' Vic waved an arm.

'I'm just a poor boy; I need no sympathy.'

Derryck moved me away. 'Sings as if he's in church. Shame he didn't take a vow of silence.' He pointed to the smallest and oldest man in the group. He was possibly fifty, with a bald head, long grey hair at the sides, with a long grey moustache and beard. He held a junior bow, like the one I used to shoot squirrels with as a boy. This one had Norse runes engraved into it.

'This is Arthur Day,' said Derryck. 'Reckons he's from a long line of a Vikings. Keep hold of your sword when this man is around.'

'Why,' I asked. 'Is he a mercenary?'

'No, he's a thief. But don't worry, he doesn't steal from the poor on principle.'

Arthur raised his tankard. 'On the principle they've got fuck all worth nicking.'

I would have replied, but I was fascinated by the jerky movements of the young man next to him. His twitch seemed to shoot up from the earth, through his feet, divert at his neck, and exit out the end of his fingers.

'You'll get along with this guy,' said Derryck. 'He reckons his ancestors were Roman, speaks a bit of Latin as well. He's going to be our Italian cook, even though he suffers from St. Vitus Dance. We call him Rigalaroni Tony.'

I shook his hand. 'Pleased to meet you.'

Rigalaroni Tony kept shaking. Derryck eventually pulled me away. 'He's very lucky to be here.'

'Because of his illness?'

Derryck shook his head. 'Because he's useless at archery. He missed the target every single time, apart from his last shot.'

'He got a bullseye?'

Derryck shook his head again. 'He got a pheasant. Tony did his little wriggle, fired the arrow into the bushes, and got the bird. The man doing the scoring only passed him if he could take it home.' Derryck handed over a shilling and ordered ale for everyone. 'And now that we have all been chosen to join the physician's unit. Let's celebrate.'

We drank until it was dark. I would have bought everyone a drink, but unfortunately, I had lost my Kings shilling. Luckily Derryck was able to loan me one.

'What's that?' Icky Custard said pointing to the clasp on my longbow.

'Ivory. From the tusk of an elephant.'

'What's that?' Icky asked.

'Well, it's ten times the size of an ox, with a nose that can move like an arm, ears the size of shields, feet that can crush a man…' I didn't want to sound like an absolute tool, so I thought I would keep it more on their level. 'And it has the biggest penis in the world.'

Now everyone moved closer. 'How big?'

'Over six foot.'

The men were impressed.

'That's the same length as the King,' said Rigalaroni Tony.

'Its impressive for any man,' Vic Flange replied.

I told them about the elephant at the tower, the lions, and a polar bear that used to swim in the Thames. We got a fire going outside. After a few more drinks we said we were ready to fight for England. Well, ready to get paid to help others fighting for England. By the end of the night, I felt as though I had formed a bond with my new comrades in arms. It was not until the next morning when I woke up in the middle of a muddy field that I wondered if I had done the right thing, and where my letter and all my money had gone.

Chapter 5

It seems to me that poverty is an eyeglass through which one may see his true friends.
   Geoffrey Chaucer, The Canterbury Tales.

We were sent to All Hallows church. While choirboys sang, I said a silent prayer for my father. Pieshop joined me, although I don't know who he was praying for. When he finished, he looked at me.
   'Do you want to be a physician?'
   'I don't know,' I replied.
   'You couldn't get into the archery regiments?'
I thought that as I was in a church I would try to be as honest as possible. 'I could have, but this unit sounded easier.'
Pieshop stared at me. 'So, you have the talent to be a physician if you set your mind to it, but you can't be bothered with all the studying. You could fight for your country, but you don't want to put in the training. You could even make something of your life in any sphere, but you don't have the discipline to do the work. It seems to me you are not fulfilling your potential.'
With that little sermon he got up and left. If he wasn't built like the leg muscles of a lion, I would have told him to poke it.
   I followed Vic Flange as he walked around admiring the internal architecture and the paintings on the walls while Derryck tried to sell a priest some bottles of white communion wine. Icky and Tony waited by sleeping in the pews. Every so often Tony's leg would raise up and shake. Arthur was the only

one who did not enter the hallowed ground as he said he wanted to remain true to his Viking beliefs.

By the third canticle the church was filled with a few hundred people. We had all been conscripted, although none of us knew what our orders were, or where we were going. I had my bow, strings, a backpack with a cloak to wear at night, and a wooden bowl. I had no idea how big the English army was, and how many people were needed to keep it moving. Word came from the back, 'Look lively, the bosses have arrived.'

The Duke of Earls Court walked up to the pulpit and read out the indenture we had all signed. We had joined the English army for an initial period of three months, meaning we should be free in time to bring in the harvest. The call had gone out to all parts of England for soldiers and would take weeks to complete, then there was the armour that needed to be made, and getting all the supplies ready, meaning those in London will have the longest amount of training. Somewhere in the speech was mention of being kept on for a further three months if the battle had not finished. The army was going to be split into divisions and their training would be at various cathedrals all over the country. Pieshop saw a banner of a yellow saltire on a blue background.

'St. Albans Cathedral. Anyone been there?'

'I have,' said Arthur, who crawled out from under a pew and dusted himself down. 'I lived a few miles away in a little village called Boreham Wood.'

'Are the locals friendly?' I asked him.

'Well,' said Arthur, 'They once beat up a man for having a book.'

'What was it?' I asked. 'Some blasphemous tome on religion, a pamphlet to bring down the monarchy, a call for political revolution?'

'No,' said Arthur. 'The people of Boreham Wood don't take too kindly to books. The poor guy hadn't even finished colouring it in.'

Perhaps it would be better to avoid this village altogether. We started to march.

St. Albans cathedral was situated twenty miles north of London. It would be the furthest away from home I had ever been in my life. We travelled along the bank of the Thames until we reached the river Fleet. From here we marched up to Watling Street. The Roman Road had been built a thousand years ago. It seemed to know we were soldiers, for the weather held as we marched in a gentle rhythm, our Longbows tapping a steady beat. Arthur asked me to carry the hamper of food he had made for the journey. He must have got it while we were in church; although, strangely, it had the crest of the Duke of Earl's Court on the side.

As we walked, Vic Flange told me about the ancient tracks that covered England which were even older than Roman times. The native English set out these routes to meet for their religious festivals, which were thousands of years older than the time of Christ. I found this impossible to believe, but Vic said there were giant stones in the west country, and they could map the stars and the sun throughout the year. I had not read any of this. Vic replied that a lot of English history was not found in any book.

'You know quite a lot about the world,' said Derryck.

'I learnt it from my old partner rambling Sid Rumpole. He also taught me to play the Lute.'

'Can you play Greensleeves?'

'What's that?' Vic asked.

We stopped marching.

'It's the most famous song in England,' said Pieshop.

'They reckon it was written in Camelot,' said Arthur. 'As the lady of the lake gently raised her arm to reveal the majestic sword of Excalibur.'

'It's played in every brothel I've ever been in,' said Icky Custard.

Rigalaroni Tony thrusted a massive twitch, causing his ladle and pans to clang. 'It's a foot tapper.'

Vic shook his head. 'Can't say I've ever heard it.' He started walking again, and we followed, all whistling Greensleeves under the midday sun until a general shouted at us to shut up.

We kept along Watling Street until the walls of London were far in the distance. The heat dried our mouths. At the springs of Stanmore, we refilled our water pouches. We travelled down to Elstree. The village of Boreham Wood was nearby. I noticed that Arthur moved into the centre of our group at this point, as he did not wish to run into the local magistrate. A drunken shaggy man with bright ginger hair and a ginger beard was shouting out if anybody wanted some. What he had to offer I was not quite sure. Herpes?

'Who's that?' I asked.

Arthur looked. 'The ginger haired bloke. That's Brownie. The local drunk.'

Why they called him "Brownie" I did not wish to know. Perhaps he was named after his fingers. I watched as Brownie picked his nose and rolled the bogie across the forehead of a young child. 'What does a drunken reprobate like that do in Borehamwood all day?'

'He's the local magistrate,' Arthur replied.

We went past the Roman brick fields of Radlett, the ponds of Park Street, and then we saw it.

St. Albans cathedral stood about three miles away on the top of a hill. These giant stone ships orbited the earth, acting as a beacon for any pilgrim to find their way. Vic told us that the original settlement was called Verulam. There was a pagan temple that used to be on the hill. When the Romans arrived, they built their own fort at the bottom of the hill, letting the Pagans continue to practice their religion. After a few hundred years the pagan religion merged with the Romans, while the new religion of Christianity was banned.

A wealthy trader called Alban lived in the town. One night three Christians, who were on the run, asked for shelter. Alban let them stay in his home and they told him about Christ. When the Romans came, Alban pretended to be one of the Christians for the leader to escape. At the trial he revealed himself to be just an Englishman. The Roman judge decided that as Verulam had pretended to be a Christian, he should be willing to die like one as well. And so, they took him to the ruined pagan temple at the top of the hill, put him on his knees, and cut off his head because he had stood up for what he felt was right.

'He must be kicking himself now,' said Derryck. 'I bet the house prices around here are pretty steep.'

We marched up Holywell Hill then onto the green near the cathedral. Those in the physician's regiment were ordered to line up. We were to be put into smaller units. Each unit would be trained to do specific jobs. As I looked down the ranks, I uttered those immortal words that anyone with an arsehole boss has repeated a thousand times over.

'Aah, fuck.' The man walking towards us was Lord Norman Farquar, the same odious bully who had tried to blame me for opening the lion's cage. I explained to Tony how I knew him.

What a weasley piece of shit,' said Tony, and gave a quick shuffle.

I tried to hide as Farquar stood in front of us.

'Name and profession.'

'Pieshop. Carpenter.'

'Pie Shoppe?'

'No. Pieshop.'

Norman slapped Pieshop's large chest with his red leather gloves. 'Watch your tone, or I'll have you in the stocks for a week.'

Pieshop could have easily told him to do one and walk away, but for some reason he never. Farquar moved on. Arthur the oldest of the group, with sweat dripping from his long hair and grey beard, was next.

'You have a face like a wizard's puddle of piss. Who are you.'

'Arthur Day.'

Farquar looked at him. 'And how did you come by that name?'

'I never do any work after lunch.'

'What's your profession?'

'Barber and dentist.'

'I wouldn't let you cut the hair of the balls of my worst enemy.' Farquar turned to Derryck. 'Are you his imbecilic grandson?'

Derryck curtsied. 'I haven't had a drink all day, your honour. Derryck's the name, Derryck Hollins, chandelier cleaner to the rich and famous.'

'That's quite an exclusive job. Which luxury estate do you live on?'

'The Saladin Estate, Peckham.'

Farquar sneered. 'Do you know why working-class scum such as yourself take an instant dislike to me?'

Derryck thought for a moment. 'It saves time?'

'No,' Farquar replied. 'It's because they quickly grasp I am a superior species. From now on, remember your place.' Derryck looked around his feet. Farquar moved on to Vic. Vic held out his hand.

'How do, Vic Flange.'

Farquar shook hands, then quickly pulled away. 'What do you do for a living?'

Vic tapped the lute that was hanging from his side. 'I like to play with myself in front of children.'
Farquar sneered. 'Then you should have joined the priesthood. Do you know what comes before Farquar?'
Vic shrugged, 'Far Diddly?'

'No, it's Lord, and don't you forget it.' Farquar moved on to Icky Custard.

'What's your problem?'

'I come from Liverpool.'

'Well don't.' Farquar noticed Tony, whose twitching became worse the longer Farquar stared.

'He's got a terrible affliction,' said Icky.

'He's from Liverpool as well?'

Tony shook his shoulders. 'St. Vitus Dance, my lord. Had it since I was a child.'

'Is it contagious?'

Tony gave a wobble. 'Only when I do the conga.'

Farquar stepped back. 'This is probably the worst bunch of men I have ever come across in my life.' He saw me. 'You.' Farquar pushed everyone out of the way. 'Well, well, well. It's the little turd nugget from the tower of London. I bet you thought you had escaped justice.'

I remained silent.

'I'm going to fiddle with you like a conker in my pocket,' he continued. 'I'm going to make sure every day is a living hell for you. Do you remember when we last met. The King was playing tennis in the great room, and I stopped you outside and said we would meet again. Do you know what happened when I went back to help service all the kings' men?'

'You got slapped in the face by a load of balls?'

Farquar shook his head. 'No. I demanded to be in charge of whatever unit you were put in. That's how much clout I have with the King.' Farquar turned to an old general who was standing nearby. 'I usually have to search high and low for all the dim-witted criminals and cripples for the nasty jobs, but fate has just made things so much easier. Congratulations gentlemen. You are going to be the latrine unit. From now on you will empty all the piss pots and shit buckets for the whole of the English army.'

As he walked away laughing, I knew the rest of the team were not going to be impressed.

'Bang goes any chance of getting my weasel greased tonight,' said Icky. 'After this lot have finished taking a dump, I bet I couldn't even get laid in Luton.'
Derryck agreed. 'Blimey. His lordships a right charmer. Like squeaky shoes on a polished floor. Five minutes and he's already doing my crust in.'

We collected our weapons of war, wooden handled shovels. We were also given our own tunics. Whereas every other man had tunics with the three lions of England, ours were black, with a white cross on the chest. Pieshop said they were old Knights Hospitaler tunics left over from the crusades. We set up our tent at the bottom of the hill near part of an old Roman wall. The river Ver ran nearby. There was also a carp lake which the monks used for food during the winter. The only good thing was that a brand-new tavern had been built nearby. *The Fighting Cocks* had everything the modern drinker could want, a long bar, food, an indoor pit to watch the fighting and a board to put up the betting odds.

We also had another stroke of luck in that Dr Culpepper was going to be our physician. When he found out I had some medical knowledge of animals and could read Latin he offered me a job working as his assistant. As I had just given my new friends the worst job in the whole of the English army, I respectfully declined. I hoped this would make me liked by the others, but it seemed to do the opposite. Derryck said I was a wally and I should have gone for it. Icky said I was being mardy. I said that I would speak to Farquar in the morning and tell him that if my mates were given different jobs, I would be his serf.

   I went to sleep that night listening to Tony shaking his restless legs, Arthur passing wind as if he was guiding a ship through the fog, and Icky going into the bushes to relieve himself every hour. Tomorrow I would do the right thing, the thing that separates the men from the boys, the thing that proves my strength of character, the thing that God created me for as long as I didn't oversleep.

Chapter 6

I've got arms that long to hold you.
  The Beatles, Please Please Me.

I woke up late. Fuck. I went up the hill to find Lord Farquar to tell him if he let the others off, I would be his servant. Because I was fifteen it would mean he would be my parental guardian. The school next to the cathedral was founded in 950 AD, over four hundred years before I was born. It had originally been part of the cathedral gate house. It was then extended to educate the sons of wealthy merchants. They had been moved out to accommodate the dukes, lords, and generals as they played war games. I went through the servant's door. The place seemed empty, so I decided to have a look around before seeing Lord Farquar.

I walked I found a library. Rows of shelves, each one filled with manuscripts from all over the world. Fantastical places I could only dream of visiting in my imagination: Athens, Cairo, Slough. So many books. How wonderful to be able to choose a different subject to read every day of the week. Perhaps if I ended up staying here it would not be so bad. I stopped when I heard a girl's laughter in the next room. Another door opened, and above the rows of books I was put under the spell of the most beautiful woman I had ever seen. She was sixteen. Her eyes shone like a thousand stars. Her smile grabbed my heart. She moved as if God was holding her in his arms. This magical moment also began my lifelong love affair of breasts and bottoms. She stopped behind a row of shelves.

'Why are you here?' Rebekah looked at me. Then realising I was clearly not one of the students, nor one of dukes that had been billeted upstairs, she gave a sensuous smile as if we had both been caught out.

'I can read and write,' was my reply.
She moved like a cat, walking around the shelves until she stood in front of me. 'Who are you?' Those eyes. Jesus. I had never understood what troubadours sang about until now. Every line of her body seemed to be calling for me to get down on my knees and thank God I was a man. Yes, she reminded me of my mum alright. I continued to remain in a gormless trance.

'Are you with my uncle Arthur?' She came towards me. 'He told me there was a gormless boy with him (I nodded). One that had met the King, who could read and write, and was handsome. Have you come to rescue me?'
I looked into this young damsels' eyes, shining like sapphires in the snow, and shook my head. 'No, I'm here to collect the piss pots.'

The other girls stood in the doorway laughed. She hushed them.

'They say you need strong hands,' her words rested on my ears like the kisses of an angel. 'Otherwise, you might get someone all hot and wet. Would you like me to show you how do it for the first time, then you can have a go yourself.'

Even though I had no idea what she was talking about, I understood why men had built cathedrals, painted great works of art, built museums and roads, and went to war. Someone had written that God was a celestial clock maker, and everything had to fit perfectly to work in harmony. Her body moved the same way as the universe.

'Good luck boy,' she said as she handed me a wooden bucket. 'The Duchess had rhubarb crumble last night. That stuff makes her pass through the eye of a needle.'

I decided to say something suave, witty, and sophisticated, 'No doubt her camel too.'
Rebekah looked at me. 'You've seen her Camel toe?'
There was an awkward silence.
She looked around. 'Where are the rest of your mates?'

'I got them into a bit of trouble with Lord Farquar, so I thought I should do the first job and let them have a lie in.' I changed tactics. 'How did you know I was with your uncle Arthur.'
She gave me a smile. 'I told you. He said the boy was handsome.' She moved closer. 'Now, I wasn't supposed to be in the sunroom, and you weren't supposed to be in the library; so, let's just keep it our little secret.'
It really was the most beautiful smile I had ever seen. No painting would ever be able to replicate it. The image of this moment I can still recall all these years later. I could have kissed her right then.

The spell was broken when Pieshop appeared. He had told Lord Farquar we were all going to stay in the unit. We were a team, and that was that. I spent the day emptying bed chambers and deciding to give this army life a try for the next couple of months.

The next morning, Pieshop got me out of the tent while the others were still asleep. He told me I was going to read every day. Not a problem. I could do that lying down. I was also going to get up early and chop wood. Not sure about that one, it was the hottest June in years. I was going to practice archery. I had him there, as I was already good. The longbow could also be used as a staff, and I would be trained in that. He was also going to carve me a sword and I was going to learn how to use it. And he was going to teach me boxing. What was I practicing for? To be better than the man you were yesterday, he replied. Who was I going to fight? Hopefully no one, but a man who doesn't know how to fight is useless, while a man knows how to fight and doesn't is virtuous.

He handed me some linen strips and told me to wrap them around my knuckles. As a kid we used to have tear ups, so I thought I could handle myself, and punching Pieshop in the palms didn't seem too bad. It was only when Pieshop also wrapped bandages around his knuckles that I realised he might want to punch back.

Even though we were assigned to be the latrine unit, we were still expected to know how to build tents, practice archery, and march with a full kit on our backs. Pieshop was a carpenter. "Measure twice, cut once", was his motto. I wondered how many men he had sized up with two looks and then cut them down with one blow. Vic Flange used to be an iconoclastic painter, covering the inside of churches with figures from the Bible, although he was no Andrei Rublev. He gave up when the merchants paying for his work kept demanding that the religious figure look like them. Instead, he became a musician. He would talk about the river Ver, how it was a chalk stream filled with different fish, which we would catch, along with rabbits and squirrels. Tony would cook, using herbs picked by Icky, who was always going into the bushes. Derryck became friendly with the monks, who always liked a dodgy deal. Arthur would usually be found in The Fighting Cocks, losing money by betting on an angry pigeon.

The doctor we would be working for was Dr Culpepper. He was a nice old guy who only joined up to stop a Duke from taking over his land. He agreed I could borrow books from the school library. As well as reading about human anatomy, there were stories about Greek and Roman heroes. It also gave me an excuse to see Rebekah. We would walk around the carp lake or go to the market. She would say something, and I just wanted to hold her hand. I went to that school more times than if I had been a student, although it meant hiding from the little Farquar on a regular basis.

The worst time would be during archery practice. I knew I was the best in the regiment, but apart from Pieshop, the rest of the team were useless. One day Tony's arrow was so far off course he hit a carp. As such we would often have to go last, much to the amusement of the other teams. My Yew longbow and its ivory clasp also brought unwanted attention. Lord Farquar decided he would like to take a good look at it.

'You, pig fart. Give me your bow.' He reached out and took it. 'Seems a bit too nice for a peasant. Did you steal it?'
I shook my head. 'It belonged to my father.'

'Is he in prison?'

'He's dead.'

Farquar smirked. 'Leprosy of the trouser sausage?' He pulled the line back. 'Could be a beauty in the right hands. I think I will keep this.'
Pieshop came over. 'It belonged to his father.'
Farquar held on to the longbow. 'What the hell do you think you are doing?'
Pieshop stepped forward, his chest almost pushing into Farquar's nose. 'It's a sin to blaspheme...and to steal' He looked like an old knights templar who had spent too long under the Jerusalem sun. Even the monks were scared of misquoting the Bible in front of him.

Farquar looked again at the longbow and then handed it back to me.

'I have a special job for you boy. Be at the school just after sunset.' He walked off.
We finished our practice. I was so distracted I scored a bullseye. Tony got a duck. He plucked it and we had it for dinner.

That evening Farquar was waiting for me outside the school.

'The Duke of Boycie is arriving in the morning; I want you to have this completely empty by then.' He waved towards the school cesspit. In the last twelve months teenage boys had filled it to the brim with their depraved ablutions. A thick crusty layer of cunk sat on the top. Once broken, the funk of excrement, sweat, crusty socks and love semolina, bored its way into your nose and throat. Farquar handed me the smallest bucket in St. Albans. 'You will dump it all on the other side of the lake. Failure to have the cesspit thoroughly emptied by morning will be seen as a dereliction of duties.' He smiled as he walked away.

Rebekah came over.

'Most of us think he's the twizzle on the end of an old monks nob.'

I nodded, wondering what sort of religious education she had been given. She looked around. 'I've got to go out tonight. I've got a secret. You can't tell anyone else. You must promise.' She looked around again. 'I'm a Lollard.'

'Well,' I replied, 'I had noticed you were a bit slow to laugh at some of my jokes, but I just thought it was down to a lack of education.'

'No,' she held my arm. 'Lollards. We believe Christianity is a spiritual concept, that a priest cannot forgive our sins, and the Bible should be available in English.' She handed me a second bucket. 'I will pray for you.' For the first time she kissed me gently on the cheek. It felt like being brushed by a feather dancing on the breath of God. She went back inside. It took me five minutes to get my breath back. That cesspit was really kicking up a stink.

In that warm summer night, my body became a salty Jerusalem for every crusading bug in the county. The sluice was half a mile away, down a hill, across the lake, past part of an old Roman wall, tip the bucket, and then it was half a mile back up to the cathedral to start all over again. Impossible to finish in one night. As I started my Herculean task, I heard movement. Arthur came out from under a cart. He dusted himself down and then pulled out a wooden wheelbarrow. Derryck came out of the moonlight shadows with another wheelbarrow. I turned to see the rest of my friends, all with wheelbarrows.

Vic put a chalk line at the tip of the gunk and placed an hourglass next to the wall. When all the sand reached the bottom, we could judge how long it would take to empty the cesspit. It took six turns of the hourglass. By the time I heard the birds singing I was done. I washed in the stream then went back to the tent to sit around a fire.

'I think that Rebekah has got a thing for you,' said Icky Custard.

I nodded.

Icky stared at the embers. 'She's a milf.'

'Milf?'

'Maiden I'd Like to…Thank heavens for breakfast.'

Tony came over with the sausages.

Rather than speak to Icky about womanly love, which I knew would end with some sort of sordid depraved act, I turned to the others. 'How do I make my next move?'

'Be honest,' said Derryck.

'Fall in love with her soul as well as her body,' said Vic.

'Be a man,' said Pieshop. 'Be a gentleman, and be an Englishman.'

Icky dipped a sausage into his mug of nettle tea. 'And as soon as you get the chance, tickle her minge. It's not the dark ages anymore lads, women have needs to. Have a butchers at this' He reached into his pocket. God knows what I was expecting. Out came a small leather-bound manuscript.

There were illustrations and tapestries of naked women, either doing various things, or having various things done to them. I studied each page. There was writing under one picture. Icky asked me what it said. I tried to read the Latin words.

'I think she must belong to a choir, as it says she's an expert on oral.'

'What about this one,' asked Icky as he pointed at an early medieval depiction of couples playing leapfrog. 'Does it say, "Mother and child?"'

I looked at the words. 'Close. It says, "Mother and Daughter". Where did you get these from?'

'Just picked them up, here and there. The last one is good.' Tony joined us as I went to the back page. The image was that of a comely wench. But what caught my eye was the man standing next to her.

'Jesus Christ,' Tony said. 'Why is he holding an elephant's penis. Is he going to pick up buns with it?'

The others also wanted a look. Vic Flange knew a thing or two about art.

'The secret of any great nipples, is that they follow you around the room.'

Maybe he didn't.

It would seem that to complete my manly duties, I would need to have Rebekah staying completely still with her eyes wide open, and for me to have a love mast with all the girth and veiny knottiness of a Spanish sailor's forearm. Romance was not as easy as I had first thought.

Chapter 7

Never in the field of human conflict was so much owed by so many to so few.
   Winston Churchill. Speech to the House, 20th August 1940, during the Battle of Britain.

The physician's camp was visited by the Duke of Boycie, his wife Marlene, and their dog. They were shown around the cathedral by the monks. Pieshop managed to join them when the duke heard about his military career. After this they were taken to the school, where Pieshop got Rigalaroni Tony the job of taking Marlene's pet dog for a walk. This was concerning as Tony's record of looking after animals was about as good as King Herod's record of babysitting. When I went to tell Farquar I had completed my task, Dr Culpepper was telling the duke and his wife I had emptied a cesspit in the dark all by myself. Farquar was silently seething.

   'What's your secret?' The Duke of Boycie asked me. 'How did you manage to obey an order so efficiently?'

   'Teamwork,' I replied, then added, 'Thanks to working with others, I have learnt how to push myself harder when coming from behind, sire.'

   'Aah yes.' said the Duke. 'The spit that lubricates every hole. Teamwork is just the thing we need in the army. Helps build morale.'

This seemed to light up Farquar's spotty face. 'Perhaps we should have a football match, just to get everyone to feel part of a team.' Farquar then said that my unit should play his.

The Duke seemed to think that this was a good idea. I was not so sure.

In 1415 football was illegal in most towns and villages due to its violence, with spectators often getting as many injuries as the players. Now Farquar wanted to see his own fully trained crack commando squad, go up against the biggest losers in the camp…us. I had played a bit of football and had seen kids taking headers with hedgehogs, bones broken, stabbings, a goalkeeper crucified, the usual Sunday kick-about. The men's game was far more serious.

For some bizarre reason, rather than play in St. Peters Street, Farquar wanted the duke and his friends to be able to see the game. As such, we would be playing football in a field. Farquar also had the strange idea of using chalk and limestone to mark out a pitch.

From their changing marquee his lordships servants appeared, all wearing the blue and yellow livery of the family Farquar's, emblazoned with the motto "*ut alii laborandum*".

'What does it mean?' Derryck asked.

'Make others work harder,' Vic replied. 'I hope they like the motto I've stitched onto our tunics, "*noli te nothi exterreant.*"'

'What does that mean?'

'Don't let the bastards grind you down.'

Icky Custard was the only one who had played football on a regular basis in Liverpool and had the missing teeth to prove it. He gave us his captains team talk.

'This going to be a game of two halves, lads, with a pitch invasion at the end. Their star player is a German, so watch it when he raises his right arm. Arthur, you've got a bit of Viking blood in you. I've made you centre forward, plenty of attacking and stealing the odd goal. Tony, I want to see a bit of Italian flair in midfield with lots of dribbling, preferably not from your mouth. Derryck don't forget the five D's on the wing: dodge, duck, dip, dive, and dodge. Vic, play defence the same way you play the lute, I want to see pain on their faces. Harry, stay in goal, out of harm's way. And Pieshop, just crack as many skulls as you can.'

Lord Farquar, the home team's manager, had also given himself the job of referee. Before he blew the whistle in what was listed as a friendly match, his goalkeeper decided to show the warm hand of harmony by running up and knocking Arthur spark out. As referee, Farquar decided to warn the unconscious Arthur that he was wasting time as they carried him away.

The match began. The pitch was hard, baked by the sun. The grass as short as the sheep could manage. Men pushed and shoved as they tried to control a pigs bladder that had been blown up and wrapped in leather. The other team did everything they could to avoid Pieshop. The German player, Herr Egrowler, broke away from the ball and ran towards me. I held out my hands, Herr Egrowler came up and dropped kicked the bladder between my legs. I went down like a sack of plums. He then kicked the football into the goal to the cheers of the crowd. One nil.

As the other team celebrated, I saw Rebekah with the other maids. She could see it was all a bit one sided, until I put my hand down into my trousers and adjusted my testicles. I threw the ball limply back onto the pitch. Twenty minutes later the German scored another one. Two nil. Arthur came out and waited to be allowed back into play. Unfortunately, Farquar ignored him until just before half time. We walked off the pitch to the sound of booing, which I thought was a bit harsh from the referee.

In our dressing tent Icky gave us mugs of hot beverage. It had a strange taste.

'Lions Main Mushrooms,' said Icky. 'Plus a few other things. To make you a bit livelier. It's like a plague pit out there.'

I looked at the white powder floating on the top of my drink. 'What other things?'

Icky looked around before he spoke. 'The secret ingredient is crime. I had a little chat with the monks about what herbs they use to keep them awake for midnight prayers. I nicked some and slipped it in your drinks to improve your performance. It's what any good manager would do. Now, to get back into this game, we've got to take that German out.'

'Leave it with me,' said Derryck.

Lord Farquar blew the whistle for the second half. Against the odds, Vic Flange did a wonderful dribble (which may have been due to the quantity of drugs he had consumed) around the defence and went on to score. He celebrated wildly. The Lions Main certainly had worked on him as he jumped into the cheering crowd. Eventually Farquar ordered Vic to put his clothes back on. It was then that Farquar noticed Herr Egrowler was lying spread eagled on the pitch. Apparently, his face had accidentally fallen onto Derryck's fist, twice. After their star player was stretchered off, the game continued. We changed tactics and steered the ball towards Pieshop. He accidentally headbutted another player, which was unfortunate as the ball was at their feet at the time. Then he lobbed the ball high and long. Derryck ran down the wing, caught it, crossed the ball over, and Icky got another goal. Two all.

The pressure was on. The other team came close to scoring again, but it went over the bar. We continued playing a counterattack game of holding the defensive line, then pressing forward at the break. Pieshop managed to tackle every player on the other team, even when they didn't have the ball. Legs were getting tired in the heat, and there was a bit more free play. I ran out and kicked the ball up to Icky. He scored. Against all odds, we were winning. I could see Rebekah cheering with the others. Farquar made a rather unique substitution. He substituted one of his players for three others. Vic tried to complain but was pushed away. The game was due to finish at sunset. The sun was dipping below the trees. Just a few more kicks left. Farquar ordered Pieshop into goal, and me out onto the field.

'Once more unto the pitch, dear friend,' said Vic as I made my way towards the centre half. The game started again. I was kicked and punched ten times without even touching the ball. Pieshop made a good save, if only because the ball hit him in the chest. We were now just defending for our lives. Their team went for another goal. They scored. Three all. I was as sick as a Dodo. It was probably something in the tea.

They were now all over us. We barely got a kick, and we hardly got a chance to touch the ball. They ran in towards our goal. Pieshop punted the ball as hard as he could. It landed near me. I kicked it forward and kept running. Their goalkeeper spread his arms and legs as I approached. I looked at the top right corner, took aim, and kicked the ball towards the bottom left. It slammed into the back of the net. The crowd cheered. Eventually Farquar had to concede that the match was over. We had won.

We celebrated by walking down to the Fighting Cocks for some light refreshment. After three pints of ale, I was beginning to feel merry, until the landlord told me to leave his daughter Merry alone. This was the happiest I had ever been. We were loud, lewd, bawdy and boisterous. Some people go around like they are sipping soup with a fork. My friends took big gulps of life, taking a chance, not knowing if it was going to be good or bad, but doing it anyway. I saw Rebekah at the other end of the bar. I walked out of the other door and met her outside. She looked stunning.

We laughed and joked, and I knew that it was now or never. I looked into her eyes, moved closer, held her hips, pulled her gently towards me, and kissed her. Those lips. I could have kissed those lips for the rest of my life. And then something happened I wasn't expecting. Our mouths opened. Our tongues touched and moved around each other. For years I thought it was only good for licking the cake spoon. When I finally came up for air it felt as if I was made of cream.

'I want to know everything about you,' I said as I held my hands around her waist, ready to go in again.

'I don't even know your full name,' she replied.
I was stumped. I tried to remember it, but my brain was more focused on her body than anything else. Luckily, I had some help from above.

'Harry Thatcher?' A man's voice said behind me.

'Yes, that's right, thanks mate.' I went to kiss Rebekah again. A large hand gripped my shoulder and pulled me away.
'Congratulations sunshine. You're nicked.'

Chapter 8

We know not whether laws be right
Or whether laws be wrong
All we know who lie in gaol
Is that the walls are strong
And each day is like a year
A year whose days are long.
　Oscar Wilde, The Ballad of Reading Gaol

That night we were all arrested and put into jail. Apparently, Lord Farquar's gold coins and jewellery had been stolen during the football match. Farquar had blamed us, even though we had an alibi and none of the jewellery had been recovered when they searched us and our tent. We all knew this was a stitch up, but what chance did a couple of ordinary men have against the rich and powerful. Rebekah came to see how we were doing. After whispering to her uncle Arthur, she called over to me.

'Is there anything you need?'

I came up to the iron bars. 'You.'

She kissed me, to the cheers of the others, and said she would find someone to defend us.

'You lucky bastard,' said Icky.

I nodded. 'She does the most amazing thing with her lips.'

'Pucker?'

'Not yet,' I replied. 'But fingers crossed.'

We waited. With no money, it seemed impossible that we would find a barrister with the wit and fortitude to be able to defend us properly. I was to be proved correct.

St. Albans courthouse was a wooden beamed building in Bricket Road. Lord Farquar was the presiding judge and prosecution barrister. Our defence barrister was a crusty old travelling performer by the name of Reginald Kincaid. Rebekah had found him being thrown out of The Boot pub for urinating into a bowl of gruel. The landlord was eating it at the time. As well as putting on morality plays, Kincaid claimed to have some legal knowledge as a circuit magistrate, due to the many, many, hours he had spent being held in custody. Unfortunately, he was also a lascivious lech, a compulsive gambler, a fornicator of loose women, a drunkard, and a golfer.

During the opening speeches he promptly fell asleep. When asked how the defendants wished to plead, he replied that it usually works better if they did it while on their knees. I volunteered to be cross examined first. The Duke of Boycie sat in the public gallery. Farquar, dressed in black robes, placed his hand on the holy Bible.

'Before I pass sentence on the deceased, sorry, defendant, is there anything you wish to say?'

If it pleases your lordship,' I replied. 'I am still waiting for instructions from my council.'

Reginald Kincaid stood up. 'I object, your honour.'

'Are you not the defendant's council?' Farquar asked.

As Kincaid sat back down, he farted so violently the Duke of Boycie's dog ran away. I raised my hand. 'I am willing to have a trial by combat. An archery competition. If I win, we are all innocent. If I lose, I shall say I am guilty.'

Farquar gave a broad grin. 'The court accepts your plea. And my I remind those in the gallery, the punishment for theft is a slow horrible agonising death in public, and I will allow for the sale of toffee apples at a reasonable price.'

The crowd cheered. Reginald Kincaid, a man who knew when he had been beaten by a great legal mind, stood up and bowed. A gentle fart let the judge know that the court was still in session.

The next day we met at Aubrey Park in Redbourn. There was a slight breeze running from left to right. I had my bow, but no string. In a corner of the field, Farquar oversaw the building of a team gallows, next to the helter-skelter and the children's face painting table. My friends were pulled out from the back of a cart. Derryck shook his head.

'Blimey Harry. Have you gone bolo? We've seen you practice. A Welsh beef farmer has got more chance of his load hitting a bull's eye than you.'

'Don't do it, son,' said Arthur. 'I will say it was me; and with my Viking blood I could escape and sail to Norway.'

'What Viking blood?' Derryck asked.

'I can trace my family line back to Hagar the Hairy, the Pox Faced pig wrestler from Wigan.'

'Who was that?'

'Well, it was my mum,' said Arthur, 'But that's not the point. I'll take the hit for you lot to get out.'

'Try to stay calm,' said Rigalaroni Tony. 'He then shook so hard his trousers fell down.

The guards handed me a line of hemp string for my longbow. It was soaking wet. I would have to pull it back even further to get enough power. Rebekah came over with a pouch of flour, which I rubbed into the string.

'Everyone wants you to win,' she said.

I was quietly confident. 'I think I may surprise people, especially Farquar. Back in the east end of London they used to call me the Crafty Cockney.'

'Why?'

'I lived in Watford. Is Farquar any good?'

'He was archery schoolboy champion three years running,' replied Rebekah. 'Won the Southeastern counties championships last year. Got to the national finals this year. He could have been a contender. Archery is the only thing he's really good at. It's almost a gift.'

Aah, bollocks. Now I wasn't so confident. Rebekah kissed me. 'Good luck.'

It seemed as though being fifteen years old in fourteenth century England was a series of desperate lows similar to being stuck under a cow with explosive diarrhoea, and momentous highs such as a kiss from your first love.

A nice crowd had gathered. Many people had taken the day off. Anything connected with an imminent horrible death always drew the families in. I waited for my arrows. You need to know are they straight, is their weight balanced, are the feathers good quality, have they been tied correctly, is the tip sharp enough. I was given three arrows. They were bog standard; in that they had been recovered from a bog after someone had already practiced with them. The tips were Bodkin style steel points that could pierce armour. Good for battle but in archery practice their heavy weight tended to make the arrow drop. Second hand arrows are also in danger of the feathers coming apart while in flight. These feathers were damp. I dared not handle them too much for fear of them falling off.

As I looked down the shaft to determine how true they were, Farquar approach. He was wearing a green bodysuit, with a green brocade hat. His bow was of good quality, but it was very thin, made more for practice than a real hunt. I noticed that his arrows were all new. They had barbed heads, which helped them fly level for longer without having to use all your power. Farquar wetted his finger and held it up to the wind.

'Going on a date with a tall man?' I asked.
Farquar smiled. 'Put the target to fifty yards.'
I watched as two men lifted the straw target and moved it back several paces. The target had a white outer ring circle, then a black ring, then blue, and a small red circle in the centre. You got one point for landing in the white area, two points for the black, three for blue, and six points for a bullseye. Standard rules. It's only the arrows still in the target at the end that count. If it's a draw, you play until the next arrow wins.

Farquar went first. He put on a goatskin leather glove, took out an ash tree shaft stitched with fine white goose feathers, pulled back his line, took aim, and let fly. There was a swish as the arrow pierced the air like a kestrel catching its prey. The arrow landed in the black. He had been overconfident. Two points. He tried to complain that it was Arthur's coughing that put him off, but the Duke of Boycie reminded him that he had agreed to the conditions.

I stepped up. Of the three arrows I took the one I thought was not the best nor the worst. My bow was stiff. It needed waxing. The damp hemp cut into my fingers. I remembered my father telling me that I shouldn't worry about all these external problems and just focus on my aim. I pulled the arrow back, aimed at the bullseye, raised the arrowhead slightly, gave a silent prayer, and fired. A puff of flour bounced off the string. The arrow shot through the air. I watched it rising, and then I realised that it was not only was it rising, but it was also veering to the right. It completely missed the enormous straw target and kept going until there was a scream. I heard Icky Custard moan, and not in his usual good way from the bushes. The arrow had just missed the Duke of Boycie's Great Dane. The dog picked up the arrow and ran away with it. Nul points.

Farquar called for the target to be moved back by fifty yards and lined up for the second shot. Arthur kept coughing. Tony kept jiggling. Farquar aimed, took his time, and fired. I watched as the arrow hit the blue on the right-hand side of the bullseye. There was a gentle clap from the invited audience. Arthur coughed again.

'Wanker,' said Tony, before taking another shake.
I will admit the weather was working in my favour. The choice of a thin bow and arrows made it easier for Farquar to steady his aim; but the wind was carrying his chances of an easy victory away.

I put some more flour on the string, hoping it would absorb any moisture and improve the tension. I looked at the two remaining arrows and went for the best one. All the training and the practice had come down to this. I pulled back as hard as I could and aimed slightly to the left. The arrow landed in the blue. Three points. I don't know who was more shocked, Farquar, or my friends. The score was now five – three. Farquar just had to hit the blue to win. So many things come into play during a competition, your mindset, the equipment, your opponent, the environment. One slight change in any of these circumstances can alter your whole game.

Farquar asked for the target to be moved to a hundred and fifty yards. He got ready, legs slightly apart, left shoulder forward, glancing up at the clouds as if trying to guess their speed, then staring at the target in the distance. He slowly pulled the line back, took his time, making sure his aim was good, then he let the arrow go. I watched, and watched, and watched, as the arrow flew straight and true, and landed on the bottom of the bullseye. As Farquar and his rich friends cheered, all my hopes and aspirations, all my dreams and fears, everything I loved and hated, my past and my future, were summed up by Rigalaroni Tony.

'You are in a world of shit.'

My last shot. It would be with the wonkiest and heaviest arrow. I thought of my father again. He had to risk his life every day doing a job that paid very little. We had started going to archery practice together when I bought my first bow at the age of seven. Even though he had worked hard all week, we went out every weekend to practice. He would let me sit inside read while he worked outside in the rain just to put food on the table. He was proud when people remarked that I had a good eye. When he died it took me months before I could pull the string back on his bow. At the tower I practiced every day, watched by the elephant and the lions. Whatever happened next could be put down to fate, random luck, skill, perhaps even a mixture of all three. I rubbed flour onto the string, then poured the last of the flour over the arrow feathers. Taking a deep breath, I straightened my left arm and pulled the string back with my right. I looked down the arrow shaft, beyond the bow, and then at the target a hundred and fifty yards away. Time became a spinning flat circle. All I had to do was let go. Just let go. Just let go.

The arrow zipped past my ear. The string sang as it vibrated. I watched as the arrow rose slightly but stayed true. There was the moment before the hawk catches its prey where the world stops. The arrow dipped. Not only did it hit the bullseye, it also knocked out Farquar's arrow. Although I heard cheering as Farquar's arrow fell to the ground, I waited to make sure my own arrow did not fall. Finally, the Duke of Boycie declared me the winner. The tournament, the trial, and my childhood were over. I ran over to my friends as the Duke told the guards to release everyone.

Farquar came over. In front of the others, he had to put on a good display.

'Congratulations. From now on, I think I shall call your unit "The Band of Bastards." Perhaps there is more to you lot than just shovelling shit.'

We celebrated in the traditional English manner by going to the pub.

From somewhere inside the Fighting Cocks, Arthur found a Viking helmet, which he insisted on wearing when he declared the day, and the pub, belonged to the Band of Bastards. We didn't mind; he was paying for all the drinks. Dr Culpepper came in and joined us. Vic picked up his lute and played a couple of songs. Freedom certainly felt good, until the landlord insisted that I leave his other daughter, called Freedom, alone.

Later that evening Rebekah and her friends joined us. The crowd was lively but good humoured. Farquar had lost his jewellery and his arrogance. These last few weeks I had gained new friends and independence. It was only when some soldiers came in with news that if we did not hear from France in the next few days, England would be at war. I held Rebekah close, not knowing how much longer we had together. With all my training I was ready to go; I just wasn't ready to say goodbye to the girl I had fallen in love with.

Chapter 9

I will live in the past, the present, and the future. The spirits of all three shall strive within me.
   Charles Dickens, A Christmas Carol.

The camp had reached the point where everyone knew they were ready. There was an element of pride at how good we were at our own jobs. We could dig out a large pit without even breaking a sweat. Every muscle in my body had grown (hopefully). Training with Pieshop showed how much I had improved since I had joined. I could fire ten arrows in a minute with ease. Archery competitions on the side brought us in a lot of prize money. I would pretend to miss the bullseye until the stakes went up. It's the only time Arthur won any money. I told him to give my winnings to Rebekah. My mind also improved.

   In those long summer nights, I would read to the others ancient tales, everything from Aesop to Zeus. The football matches in the regiment became more boisterous, causing a few injuries, but at least it gave Dr Culpepper and myself a chance to practice on bodies before the real thing came along. In return, Culpepper would come to the pub and gamble with Arthur on the fighting cocks. Culpepper used agricultural science and breeding; Arthur went by the luck of Nordic Runes and the bird's name; neither seemed to win. They decided that what they needed was their own bird they could train to fight and give a meaningful moniker. The whole regiment got involved, building our own fighting pit, rearing chickens, waiting for the big win.

One day I went with Rebekah to the clock tower. Situated in the town centre, it had been built ten years earlier in 1405 as a way of stopping the monks from having the power to regulate time keeping in the town. It faced the abbey but stood on slightly higher ground, just to annoy the monks. It was originally the site of an Elanor Cross. Twelve Eleanor crosses were constructed throughout eastern England under the orders of King Edward I between 1291 and 1294 in memory of his wife Eleanor of Castile. The site of each cross marks the nightly resting place of Eleanor's funeral procession.

We went up the steps. I'm not really a lover of modern architecture but I was fascinated by the workings of the clock. Wooden beams held a series of bronze wheels and levers which would turn and spin the hands. Rebekah's family had originally come from London but had moved out during the plague. They lived in Boreham Wood, then a cottage near St. Botolph's church in Shenley, until she got a job as a maid in the school. I told her my father had died, but not how. When we went to The Boot pub to meet the others, we found Reginald Kincaid and his group of troubadours inside. They were on their way to give a performance at Salisbury Hall near Shenley and asked us to join them. Salisbury Hall had chickens and a silkworm farm. Arthur and I insisted we go, me for the arrows, Arthur for the cock.

As we travelled through the hamlet of Shenleybury, Icky showed Reginald Kincaid his nuddy book. Kincaid claimed that one of the gentlemen in the illustrations was himself, taken many years ago when his magnificent rod could tell the time just by laying down naked on a sunny day. He claimed he was the country's greatest living actor and artists model. I didn't quite believe him. The man in the illustration had his mouth closed.

At Salisbury Hall we were all invited into the great room by the lord and lady of the manor. After telling them we were about to go off to war, they gave us food and drink and allowed us to watch the entertainment. Reginald Kincaid and the others performed the morality play, *The Pride of Life.* It was the story of a King who meets death as he tries to get home. He mistakes Death's humility as being small and weak. After being encouraged by his flatterers, the King challenges death to a fight. His wife pleads with him to let death pass on its way. But the King, believing he is more powerful than death, refuses. They meet in the field of battle. The King is dressed in his finest armour. Death is dressed in humble rags. The King struts upon the stage, playing the role of conqueror even before any victory has occurred. He recklessly charges forward in the belief that he is bigger than life and more powerful than death. He is killed, more by his own impudence than by any skill from death. The queen visits death and pleads for her husband's soul. Death agrees, as he knows the King will spend the rest of his life knowing that time is the master, and its servant death is always waiting at the end. The King returns to the stage, redeemed and penitent. Kincaid, dressed as the king, warns the audience that everything we do in life will come back to judge us in the end.

When the play was over, I asked the lady of the house for some silk to fix the feathers on my arrows. Because my hair was long, she was surprised I was an archer. I told her I was going to be a physician's apprentice and that I had worked in the royal tower. She noticed the ivory clasp on my longbow and gave me a leather pouch filled with fine thread. It was agreed we could camp in the fields and hunt for rabbits.

We went out and I shot a few coneys in the moonlight. Tony had a go and missed. When he tried to pull an arrow out of the ground he ended up with a dead mole. Arthur appeared from under a cart with a barrel of ale. Icky produced a pouch of hemp leaves, which he tried to sprinkle some on the rabbits as they cooked on the skillet. He was so drunk that a lot of the herbs fell into the fire. The smell was pungent, but for some reason we found it quite funny.

We continued to enjoy the night. Kincaid and his band of brothers joined us. The food, the drink, and the company were all good. Kincaid claimed to have met Robin of Sherwood. Poxy Loxley was an old man by then, riddled with syphilis, with a penchant for dogging in the Forest layby. Kincaid kept the myth of Robin Hood alive by creating a play about him. It sold well because so many men were about to go off on another crusade.

'I don't think there will be a war,' said Derryck, holding a grilled mole that had a broken arrow stuck up its arse. 'As soon as we get to the coast, the French will hear how big our army is, and give the land back to Henry.'

Pieshop disagreed. 'The French will not do anything until we land in France. They will measure our strength, then wait, and wait, and wait for us to become weak.'

'I still fancy going to France,' Icky chipped in. 'Just to get chocka in the brothels.'

'Me too,' said Derryck. 'Not the knocking shops, the other trade. The wine, the cheeses, and the armour. We could make a fortune and have our own empire like the Romans. Just think lads, this time next year, we could be like the legionnaires.'

'You get a ship, I will sail it,' said Arthur. 'It would be like my ancestors taking the longboats back to the fjords.'

'Cor blimey,' Derryck replied. 'You can't even handle a gravy boat. How do we know you're not just making this Viking stuff up?'

In the moonlight Arthur showed us the amulet around his neck. A silver circle with nine staves, meant to represent all the possibilities of the past, present, and future.

'You can buy those down the market,' said Derryck. 'What else you got?'

Arthur took his tunic off to reveal a tribal tattoo that covered his back. There was a bearded figure sitting on a boat, and two dogs sitting either side.
Derryck almost dropped his mole. 'Did Rigalaroni Tony do the artwork, or were you in a storm at the time?'

'I Like it.' Said Arthur, looking over his shoulder. 'It's Odin and his hounds on their journey to Valhalla. One dog looks one way, the other dog goes the other way, and this guy is saying, Whadda ya want from me? There's some runic symbols underneath, very religious, very sacred, just above my arse crack.'
Vic clambered over. 'I can read a bit of old Norse.' He looked at the symbols. 'It says the man's name is "Odeon."'

'Odeon.' Derryck asked. 'Who the fuck is Odeon?'
Vic shrugged. 'The Viking God of pictures? Where did you get the tattoo done. Denmark, Ragnarok, Norway?'

'Southend,' said Arthur. He scratched his bald head. 'I'd had a few drinks, and I did a massive beer fart. It made the tattooist cry. I thought it was because the art was so good.'

We were impressed he had such a big tattoo. Pieshop stood up and took off his tunic. Black tribal markings were stamped on his chest, back, and arms. He had got them from Razzouk while he was in Jerusalem. Some of them had come from ancient templates a thousand years old, when Christ was still alive. He pointed to one that was the Lion of Judah, another was of St. George, another was the angel of destruction. I was more interested in the large scar emblazoned on the side of his stomach. Pieshop calmly explained that when he was younger, he fought a Muslim who was a better swordsman but not as humble. He didn't elaborate, and I didn't ask further. He had already done his duty to his country. We spent a warm night under a thousand stars. I could have stayed lying on the ground forever. The ale had made my body a liquid vessel, gently moving, safe and warm, until I fell asleep.

The next morning, we said goodbye to Kincaid and headed back to camp. Arthur carried a basket which held a cockerel. He kept saying how he and Dr Culpepper were going to make a fortune fighting it. I had some rabbit pelts I was going to give to Rebekah. Walking up the hill, I noticed there were more horses and carts than usual. Outside the cathedral men packed the tents away. Perhaps Henry had called the French King's bluff and won. A messenger told us we were needed in the school. Probably another bucket that needed emptying. As we made our way past the crowd, we saw Dr Culpepper putting jars into a cart. Arthur held up his basket and called over to him.

'Doctor, do you want to take a look at my prize cock?' Dr Culpepper put down a jar. 'Not now Arthur. Just give it a wash and rub some cream on it twice a day.'

Inside the school me and Pieshop found the Duke of Boycie and Marlene enjoying breakfast.

'Are you looking forward to the fighting?' The Duchess of Boycie asked Pieshop.

'I am in the physician's unit,' Duchess,' Pieshop replied. 'The only weapons we carry are longbows. None of us have any armour. If we fight it will probably be at close quarters. I am ready to punch any French man that comes near me.'

The Duchess turned as Icky Custard came into the room. 'Aah, I was just speaking to your friend here about having a go at the French. Are you also looking forward to knocking one out as soon as you can?'

'No need, duchess,' Icky replied. 'I had a quick hand shandy behind a bush first thing this morning.'

There was shouting in the corridor.

'What is the meaning of all this?' Lord Farquar came into the room.

'We are just talking,' said the Duke of Boycie. 'Perhaps you should promote this unit from latrine duties?'
Lord Farquar looked directly at me. 'I agree.' A broad smile spread under his beaklike nose. 'I am giving you band of bastards the honour, nay, the privilege, of also being the unit that buries the dead.' Farquar grinned a toothless grin. 'I only wish I could be there to see it.'

'Then I have more good news,' said the Duke of Boycie. 'As I have to deal with matters at home, I am unable to sail. I am going to give you have the honour of taking my place in France. Congratulations gentlemen. For you all, on the 25th of July 1415, the war has finally begun.'

PART TWO

ABBEY ROADS

Chapter 10

London calling to the faraway towns
Now war is declared and battle comes down
   The Clash, London Calling.

Farquar made sure we were the last unit to leave. As I watched the carpenters and arrow makers march away, I thought about how much had changed. I had learnt anatomy from Dr Culpepper, Pieshop showed me how to fight, Tony had taught me how to cook, Icky taught me all about herbs, Vic showed me about the land, Derryck taught me about people, and Arthur would pick up anything that wasn't nailed down. The skill I showed the others was that I had learned to read at the age of five. It was that simple, and that profound. It allowed me to sit around the fire and tell stories, the ones that really mattered, of men doing great things. I was also able to read letters and orders lying around in the belief they were safe from prying eyes. Arthur knew when the school was getting barrels of cheese and ale before Lord Farquar did. We were a team, although there was another person who had made the greatest impact in these last few weeks.

I tried to say goodbye to Rebeckah. But she was nowhere to be found. Guards were placed everywhere to make sure none of us changed our minds and escaped. I helped Tony place his cooking pots on the back of a cart. He was offered a lift in the back but he gave his space to Arthur, who climbed into the back wearing his Viking helmet and holding his cock. Icky had his last dump before we left. Some of his logs were so thick and nutty I wondered if he was half bear and half squirrel.

The Knights had left first, to the cheers of the locals, followed by the knights' servants, then the horses and carts filled with the physicians' tents, then the food carts, then the medicine, then the physicians themselves. Pieshop shared out some bread and meat. Once we started marching it could be night before we rested again. I had still not seen Rebekah to tell her goodbye.

We went past the ancient Roman walls knowing that some of us might never see them again.

'I wonder what the Roman soldiers would make of all this,' said Vic.

Derrick looked over. 'Probably wondering how out of all the places the Roman empire conquered, they ended up in wet and windy England.'

'I don't know,' said Vic. 'I can imagine them on a summer night sitting around a fire, drinking wine, eating rabbit legs, and probably having a right old laugh.'

'Blimey,' Derryck replied. 'Looking at some of the brickwork, I think they must have been on the old El vino for breakfast. It's weird though, isn't it. The Romans built all these roads and walls; and then you get nothing for hundreds of years until we start building cathedrals like the one up there. My grandad told me it was called the dark ages because they hadn't invented the window.'

Vic smiled. 'It sounds like your grandad is a bit of a sage.'

Derryck shook his head. 'Not really, he hardly touches any vegetables. He doesn't even like singing Greensleeves.'

We kept marching, with Vic insisting he didn't know the tune.

We marched down Watling Street. Near the village of Boreham Wood, Brownie, the ginger haired drunk, stood with a jug of ale and kept calling out, 'May the road rise with you.' He then promptly fell backwards into a bush. We went up to the village of Elstree. In Stanmore, Pieshop refilled his pouch from the springs. He said the water here was better than the water in London. We all did the same.

It was here we were joined by some foot soldiers, and a full regiment of Welsh archers. Their faces were tanned from practicing in the sun all day. Then we were joined by another regiment of foot soldiers. Now the army must have been a mile long. The horses and carts clattered as dust rose into the air. More and more people came out to watch.

~

That evening we arrived at Hampstead Ponds. Three other regiments were waiting, including a whole field of knights. The banners and flags fluttered in unison. Hundreds of horses were walked in a large circle near the pond. It was a wonderous sight. Most of these men had marched down from Warwick Castle. Men with longbows, tunics, banners, armour, sharp steel pikes, ready to fight. It felt like a real army.

But we were the band of bastards in more ways than one. Our tunics signified no rank, no Knight, no regiment, no castle, no shire. We were not even sure they were made in England. For most people black signified death, and the white cross some even considered to be Jewish. When we told others we were the latrine unit they would laugh. We had an old man wearing a Viking helmet, a scouser who looked like he'd eaten magic mushrooms and decided to cut his own hair, a cook whose St. Vitus Dance affliction made him dangerous with a spoon, a musician who couldn't play the standards, a market trader who always seemed to end up with dodgy gear, a carpenter who didn't have any tools, and me, a cockney who could read and write, which was rarer than rocking horse shit. We were hardly a band of elite assassins. The good news was that nobody bothered to order us around. Arthur cut hair and trimmed beards and we ate apples while the generals held a meeting. The sun was beginning to wane, but the decision was made to keep moving. The plan was to get across the river and rest for the night in St. George's Fields.

With five thousand armed men loose on the outskirts of London, the plan quickly fell apart. The Knights and those with expensive items in their carts moved away first. The most enthusiastic soldiers followed. But others seemed to waddle into the pubs and brothels like a duck to water. We walked to Smithfield Market as Tony's family worked there. They welcomed us with food and drink, happy their boy had made friends and was being looked after. I thought about my own family. I thought about Rebekah and wondered if I would ever see her again, or worse, if she had met another man. They gave us some good quality salted meat. As we left, Pieshop told us to keep our money safe rather than spend it on the prostitutes that called to us from every dark doorway.

'I fancy getting my own salty sausage eaten,' said Icky as he eyed up a buxom wench sat on an upper window.

Pieshop kept us moving. 'Let's get over the bridge first.'

The next house had a sign on it. 'What does it say?' Icky asked me.

'The Crafty Butcher.'

'Sounds like a right naughty knocking shop. Do you reckon the women do a deal for anyone who works in Smithfield?'

'It's a Greek brothel,' said Vic. 'It means they sneak their meat in through the back door.'

I looked up to see a man wave at me. London was indeed a strange place at night.

We stopped at the Old Watling Inn near the church of St Peter upon Cornhill. Only Pieshop, Vic and Derryck had travelled south of the river. Bandit country. Derryck told us

London Bridge was a miniature city itself. The nineteen arches caused the river to slow down enough for it to freeze when it was cold. Some of the houses on the bridge were seven storeys high. He said a rich man could start on one side, and by the time he reached the other side he would be penniless, naked, stabbed, and riddled with the pox. We finished our drink and walked towards the Thames. When I saw the bridge in the distance I knew there was no going back.

'That's London,' said Derryck.

'It's like an elephants' penis,' said Tony. 'Smelly and wet.'

'Beautiful isn't it,' said Derryck. 'My mate Sash runs a taxi firm on this part of the river. He made his money bringing Gherkins up from Brighton for the big tavern houses.'

'Pickled?' I asked.

'He usually was by lunchtime,' Derryck replied.

We reached the church of St. Magnus the Martyr. Next to it was the gate house. I looked up to see three heads squished onto the tall spikes. The crows had pecked out the eyes. What these men had done was written on the walls. One was a traitor, the other had been a thief, and the third was accused of being a Lollard. I quickly went inside.

The guards watched us with idle interest as we went up to the desk.

'Toll,' said a round-faced man, without looking up.

'We go in the name of the King,' said Pieshop.

'The army has already been through.' He finally looked at us. 'I don't recognise your livery. Are you sure you're not just troubadours trying to get a free pass? Theres one man, Kincaid, the worm skinned turd owes me a fortune. Are you sure you're not with him?'

We said nothing. He noticed the ivory badge on my longbow. 'Hello, that's an interesting piece.' He got up from his chair and moved around the table. 'What is it?'

Pieshop ignored him. 'Come on,' he said to us all. 'Let's get a wriggle on, no offence Tony.'

'Wait,' said the man. 'I said I don't believe you are part of the King's army. What regiment has black tunics?'

'We are the Knights Hospitallers.'

The man looked surprised. 'They disappeared years ago. Why have you come back now?'

Pieshop leaned in close. 'Because we've all taken a vow to serve God after becoming lepers.'

Tony's St. Vitus dance shook through his body. Vic reached over and pinched the fat man's nose. 'Crabalocker fishwife.'

The man was not impressed. 'Seize them.'

Two guards came forward. Pieshop punched the first man. From my medical training I ascertained that his nose had been broken. That, along with the copious amount of blood running down his face, and him screaming, 'You've just broken my fucking nose.'

Tony pushed the other guard away. Two more guards came running. Derryck and Icky grabbed them and fell to the floor. I held out my longbow as if ready to use it as a staff. The fat man called out for more, until Pieshop took out his dagger and placed it at his throat. The fighting quickly stopped. Arthur came out from under the desk, brushed down his tunic and adjusted his helmet. Pieshop told the fat man to open a large wooden door.

'Go,' said the man. 'You'll have no protection on the river, not even from Hades himself.'

'We're on a mission from God,' said Tony as we passed. 'You big fat bell end.'

Outside, there was an empty walkway and another set of gates, heavy enough to stop people getting onto the bridge, and from trying to get off. Beyond that was the bridge itself. The lights and smells seemed to invite us into the depths of hell. The sound of laughing and screaming fought against the constant rush of water. Pieshop turned to us.

'Whatever comes out of those gates, we've got a better chance of survival if we work together.'

Vic Flange agreed. 'You will never find a more wretched hive of scum and villainy in the whole of London.'

A gate opened. A brassy woman ran forward.

'Del Boy,' she grabbed Derryck and gave him a big kiss. 'I thought you were in the clink?'

Derryck gave a nervous laugh. 'Hello Blossom. How's tricks?' She looked at Derryck and his black and white tunic. 'Here, what's with the outfit. You look like a chess players ring piece.'

'It's a secret,' said Derryck. 'Keep it under your hat.'

'You got a big job lined up?'

Derryck tapped his nose, 'We're doing a bit of ducking and diving to get a load of scrap metal off the government. But keep it schtum. I don't want anyone pulling my plonker.'

Blossom laughed. 'You've changed.'

As we moved forward, she continued to loudly tell everyone that Derryck was planning to nick a load of gear from the government. This seemed to make us very welcome among the locals.

When we reached halfway across the bridge, I told Tony the story of Caesar crossing the Rubicon. This was a river near Rome. Caesar knew that if he stayed where he was he would just be an ordinary Joe Blow with nothing to show in his life. If he crossed it, he would become either emperor, or be killed. He decided to go forward and let the dice of fate fall where it may. Tony was not so sure. He thought it was stupid to roll dice in a river. The south bank of London came into view. I might as well have been travelling to the other side of the world.

We made our way towards the Bethlehem Hospital. Others had already set up camp. We found a patch of grass that was not covered in horseshit. Pieshop told me to tie my longbow around my wrist and we bedded down for what was left of the night.

I couldn't really sleep. All I thought about was Rebekah. Arthur kept snoring and farting in my general direction. The man was a human set of bellows. Just before dawn I noticed Tony moving more than usual. He got up and walked through the mist. I followed. I couldn't really lose him, as every so often he would wiggle and shake like a man having a piss in Winter.

Bethlehem hospital stood nearby. It was also known as Bedlam. Here they kept all the unfortunates that society only wanted to see from a distance and laugh at. Tony stared up at the windows. The shouting and the screams from inside were not the same as those on the bridge. Tony said that if it wasn't for his family, he could have ended up in a place like this. When he was younger the other kids would take the mick by jerking around in front of him. He would run after them, and when he came back, he would find it had been a trick for the older boys to steal his stuff. He had joined up in the hope of being part of a team and making friends.

Arthur appeared, like a shit house rat. How he crept about so silently at his age I never knew. He said to Tony that he was a mate, and he would always keep an eye on him. Athur then said that I was born lucky, and the Gods must want me to be someone. We were standing in a field of horse shit and he was wearing a Viking helmet at the time, so I wasn't so sure on that one.

'Maybe crossing the Thames is you throwing the dice,' said Tony.

'That story was a long time ago,' I replied.
Tony shrugged (I think). 'Perhaps the past is never really over. Not for some people.'

We watched as the nuns made their way into Bedlam to start their next shift. The lamps they carried cast dancing shadows on the wall. Those poor sods inside probably didn't know the difference between shit and clay or sunlight and shadows. For the first time in weeks, I missed my mum.

Chapter 11

So, the days float through my eyes but still the days seem the same.
And these children that you spit on as they try to change their worlds,
Are immune to your consultations,
They're quite aware of what they're going through
   David Bowie, Changes

Morning. My body went through the monotonous motions of marching, but all I could think about was Rebekah. I was worried that she had found someone else. We marched south, towards the green hills of Wimbledon. Pieshop reckoned we would have a lot of waiting around before we sailed for France. Enough time for spies to report back to Paris. I had no idea what a spy was. Vic said they were people working for the enemy who pretended to blend in to try and defeat us. It could be anyone, from a travelling priest to the man standing in the field with his lambs asking if you wanted to stop and eat with him.

'Maybe he's a shepherd spy?' Tony shook a leg.
Icky said that if the land was in France, then it belonged to the French rather than us. Derryck argued that if we had paid for it, then the French should have bought it off us. Tony wondered why King Charles and Henry didn't just fight it out between them, rather than thousands of ordinary people having to.

We passed a small village. A crowd had gathered on the green. A man was marched up to a pile of wood and tied to a stake. The man's crime was he had been caught reading out the

Bible in English. His life was to be ended because of the words he used.

'What's he done?' Arthur asked.

'He's a Lollard.'

'He stole a lolly?' Arthur took his Viking helmet off.

'He's a Lollard. He got caught translating the scriptures into English.'

I wondered how someone could be killed just because of language. The Romans had believed in different Gods. Would someone kill me because I could read Latin. Pieshop kept us moving.

'It's not right,' he said. 'But now is not the time to do or say anything stupid.' He looked at me as he said the last bit. He must have thought I was going to run away to see Rebekah.

We reached the top of a hill. I turned to take one last look at the city. I could see some of the church towers I had climbed as a boy. Even in summer there was still smoke from all the kitchens. I hoped Rebekah was safe. We continued marching down towards the county of Sussex.

As we moved further away from London, I realised just how beautiful England was. Paths meandered around green hedgerows. Ripened berries and fruit hung from the branches. Every plant could be used by Icky for healing or Tony for cooking. There were fish in the rivers and rabbits in the meadows. Some of the trees were as wide as a house. Fields of golden wheat stood over six-foot high. Sheep safely grazed on green grass. Vic said much of the country had been this way for thousands of years. If paradise existed, it must look like England. Although I had seen many wonderful things on my journey so far, nothing compared to the village of Chillingbourne.

It was situated on the pilgrim's route to Canterbury. Thatched roofs were warmed by the sun. Tall plants shaded the cottage windows. The three local taverns had been supplied with enough ale to wet the thirst of the whole of London. And it was here that I first saw the Knights in their full finery. Horses paraded in their colours, footmen wore the uniforms of their lords, every tent flew their banners high. Some practised jousting by holding a lance and riding towards the bullseye. Another confession. Although I have read the books and seen the pictures, I have never actually ridden a horse. We had never been able to afford it. I carried on watching, wondering what it would be like to ride so high and fast. The only disappointment was that Lord Farquar had also arrived in the village. Dr Culpepper came and asked me to collect Ladies Mantle while it was in season. I journeyed into an orchard and scrumped some fruit before deciding to head back. Climbing over a gate, I saw her as she moved through the fair. She was dressed in white robes and carried a handful of Marigold's.

 I ran over, dropped my basket, lifted her up, and kissed her. Rebekah had asked Dr Culpepper for a job as a nurse. He had showed her dried plants and herbs, and she knew each one. She wanted to surprise me for my birthday. I was overjoyed, not yet realising she could also be going to France. We walked through a meadow until it was only the two of us and two cows. They watched me while I watched her. The way she wore that dress when the sun came shining through, I couldn't believe all of *that* belonged to her. She bent down and picked up a piece of fruit that had fallen from my basket.

 'Oh, what a lovely pear.'
I moved closer. 'You took the words right out of my mouth.'
I kissed her again, and tried to get her to lie down. She was happy to kiss but didn't want to get anything on her dress. We decided to go back to the physician's camp.

 When we saw Dr Culpepper, he smiled.

'She reminds me of a witch that used to be in my village. Knew every plant for miles.' He then asked Rebekah to go to the cart and collect some jars.

'I thought you would enjoy that surprise. You are a very lucky young man. Although you need to be careful.'

'Because we have slightly different faiths?' I replied.
For the first time the old doctor looked at me as if I was a young child who had asked a question, and neither lying or the truth would give an answer that both of us would be happy with. He let out a sigh. 'You saw the man burning?' He watched as I nodded, not sure of how to answer. 'She must trust you very much. If anyone else finds out she could be tortured.' I nodded again. 'She told you as well?'

'No,' he replied. 'You just did.' He went over and closed the tent doors. 'The King believes his rule will be diminished if he goes to France. He is cracking down on any political and religious dissent. I got Rebecca out of St. Albans for her own safety. Be careful of what you say, and who you say it to. Being able to read and write does not make you smart.' He finally smiled. 'God gave you two ears and one mouth for a reason. Listen more so that you will know people by their lies rather than their replies.'

I agreed, wondering if Dr Culpepper was a spy. I went back out with Rebekah and Icky to collect Yarrow. The plant was good for healing wounds, so we got three barrels worth. We also dug out the roots of the Tormentil plant, as it helped fight off stomach ailments such as dysentery. Rebekah went off to collect Henbane, Hemlock, and opium poppy seeds. She also promised me something for my sixteenth birthday. I hoped the others would not find out. They rarely needed an excuse to have a piss-up.

The next morning, we had fried goose eggs for breakfast along with bacon and warm bread. I went out collecting more herbs. For the rest of the day the others seemed to plan and plot as to what was going to happen to me. That evening, I was taken to the doors of the village church. Pieshop told the priest that the King wanted to pray in secret tonight and so needed the keys. The priest wondered why Knights Hospitallers had been given the job of royal protection. Pieshop took out a bag of coins, and his knife. Either the church key could go in the lock, or the priest's puckered penis. The priest took the money, which he promised he would give to charity.

Icky appeared with a wheelbarrow of straw, under which was a barrel of what the locals called "Cider." Arthur was behind him, wearing his helmet, with Rebekah holding his arm. She was wearing a white linen dress with a daisy chain in her hair. Her lips had been coloured with a rouge. She was a thing of beauty. Her lashes fluttered like a baby's smile. Her eyes were like the bluest skies. Her tanned cheekbones had been spun by angels. Her lips could make you feel as if you had been swallowed up by the universe. Her neck was made smooth by heavenly kisses. Her feet were carved from marble. Icky Custard stopped me.

'Whoa, whoa, whoa, sweet child of mine. You've missed out the best bits.'

Joining us were a group of nurses. Icky's eyes bulged like an old dogs' balls. The caged bird that Arthur had brought with him was boiled and served with beets and rocket salad. It may have been a third-rate fighting cock, but it was a first-rate chicken fricassee. We ate and drank as the shadows disappeared behind church walls. Around the fire Vic played his lute. We sang the songs we knew. It then turned out that Rebekah, having learnt to sing in the cathedral, also knew French and Latin songs. Icky kept remarking on her wonderful tongue control. The voice of a woman singing about the sweet sorrow of parting from a loved one made us feel melancholy and happy at the same time.

The moon rose. Orange flames flicked shadows on silver wood. I fancied another jug of ale. But that was not to be. After being given a white blanket, Rebekah took my hand. To the smiles of the women, and the smirks of the men, we walked into the church. As I closed the door behind us I could hear Vic and the women sing "Sumer is Icumen in." We walked down the aisle and up the steps of the clock tower. I didn't want Jesus or his mum to see me naked.

For many years women had been a profound mystery to me. I had grown up with a mother and older sister, but this was my second summer of feeling something stir whenever I saw an attractive woman. This was not quite true. Young, old, thin, fat, rich, poor, there were times it didn't matter. I was like a young rooster outside the hen house. I had been too shy to speak to most of them, but now I was proud of my body. I had grown taller, and in the last two months I had been digging every day…Rebekah stopped me and said I was thinking too much.

I stood between a wooden frame as a large clock wheel ticked, took my shirt off, and held on to the beams. Rebekah gave a small appreciative laugh. I thought I would do the same when she took her dress off. In the candle-light she silently let the dress fall to the floor. I could not stop staring. They say that God made man first. I can believe it. There are parts of me that look as if they have been lumped together by an amateur. But when it came to making a woman, I reckon the old rascal practiced getting it right a lot of times before he was happy. And I'm glad he did. She came over to me.

'I can't let go,' I told her.
We kissed. She ran her fingers along the line of my biceps, across my shoulders, and then gently scratched my chest. I did not move. She kissed me.

'I still can't let go,' I said. I gently kissed her naked shoulders. I kissed her neck as she purred in my ear.
Her hands reached around my waist. 'Why can't you let go?'
'Because I'm afraid that if I do, I am going to lift you up, carry you over to that bed, and explore and kiss every single part of your body for the rest of my life.'

She took my hands and put them around her waist. She kept kissing me as I picked her up and carried her to the blanket. I kissed her lips, then moved to kissing her body. I was sixteen years old, and I had never felt so alive. I could not stop kissing her. The only strange moment was when she helped take off my trousers. I had read the manuscripts and seen the pictures, but as for the actual practicality of sex, I was not sure.

I laid her down. We kept kissing. I looked at her and thought about how life is a funny thing, and then it happened. Although it did not grow to the size of an elephant's, I like to think that I could have blown my own trumpet that night. You could have used it to knock nails into a plank of wood. We were two star crossed lovers. We became one as the universe looked down on an ancient church. Then we did it again after I had got my breath back.

The next morning while Rebekah was asleep, I gently moved my arm from under her neck and went down the staircase. As I stepped out of the church, everyone was there, including the priest and the local prostitute called Charity, all cheering and clapping. I quickly went back inside to put some clothes on.

'Grown-arsed men,' said Rebekah as she put on her dress. 'Worse than children. And one of them is my uncle.'
Having plucked my innocent darling angels' sweet precious flower, I asked the question that all noble gentlemen of good breeding wish to know. 'How was I?'
She put on her shoes. 'Don't worry. Nobody hits the bullseye every time, especially if the arrows a bit wonky.'

I didn't know whether I loved her because of her sense of humour, or was petrified of it. She kissed me and went out of the church first. The others cheered again. Rebekah took a graceful curtsey, then left to go back to work. For all that I had learnt in books, you couldn't beat on the job training.

On the third of August we were told to pack. We would be marching towards Winchester to meet the rest of the army. From there we would go to Southampton, and down to sea.

Chapter 12

If you want to know what a man's like, take a good look at how he treats his inferiors, not his equals.
   J.K. Rowling, Harry Potter and the Goblet of Fire.

We marched towards Winchester. Vic said this was where Alfred the Great smoked some cakes. Icky's eyes lit up, believing they were hemp cakes. Vic explained that in 900 AD King Alfred was hiding from the Vikings (Arthurs eyes lit up) in the home of an elderly woman. Not knowing who he was, she asked him to watch the cakes she was cooking. But because he was thinking about how to save the country, he let them burn. The woman comes back and moaned at him, saying he had one job to do and fucked it up. He accepts the bollocking because she is right.

'There's a moral to that story,' said Tony. 'But I'm fucked if I know what it is.'

'Never overcook hemp cakes,' said Icky.

'Get a better stove,' said Derryck. 'My mate Monkey Harris has got a load of fire damaged ones.'

Vic shook his head. 'Always listen to women, because men are idiots.'

Pieshop stopped them. 'It's about dealing with the task in hand, no matter how unimportant you think it is, rather than dreaming about the future.'

He said something else, but to be honest I wasn't listening. I was thinking about seeing Rebekah later that night. All that talk of cakes had left me fancying a little nibble.

Winchester was where the whole of the Kings army finally met up, and where many of the Knights had been training for the last few weeks. Anyone who had a nice horse stayed in the castle and the cathedral. The soldier's barracks were in the west of the town, and the archers had the east side. Because we were skivvies, we were camped in fields about a mile away. The good thing was we could go anywhere as no one had a clue who we were, and when we did tell them they never wanted to shake our hands.

With an army of men and money, the fair had also arrived. In one field I saw the cart belonging to Reginald Kincaid next to a big marquee. There was a bear baiting pit, a tombola stall, and a bowling green. In the next field prostitutes were setting out their battle lines with military precision, waiting for the balls to roll in.

One morning Pieshop asked me to go to with him to Wolvesley Castle. Arthur asked to go as well, in case somebody needed a haircut. We found the encampment for Sir Michael Tate. He rode up and looked down at us.

'What do you want?' He held out his sword as if about to use it.

'We are part of the physician's unit, sire. We are on our way to the chapel to pray,' said Pieshop.
Sir Tate must have thought we were simpletons, but the chapel could only be reached by going through his encampment. Sir Tate placed the flat edge of the sword on Pieshop's shoulder. 'Be quick about yourselves. And if you so much as touch anything that belongs to me, I shall have you in the stocks by sunset.' With that, Sir Michael Tate trotted away without bothering to ask any more questions.

A young stable boy, no more than twelve, was feeding the horses. He stopped when he saw us.

'Dad.' He ran up and hugged Pieshop.
Pieshop spent what little time we had making sure his son was OK. His son said that the work was hard, but it was worth it because he got to ride the horses. Sir Michael Tate shouted a lot, but he never liked to ride early, and they never saw him after sunset. Pieshop told him to try and read every day, and as he was underage he could go home if he wanted. But his son replied that there might not be another war for a hundred years, and this could be the only chance to be like him. If he worked hard enough, one day he could even take part in a joust.

I remembered Spartacus, the slave who became a great general. I said that the moral of the story was that it is better to be a poor free man than a slave to a rich man.
Pieshop placed both hands on his boys' shoulders. 'Just be careful.' The boy nodded, and Pieshop hugged his son.

We decided it was time to go when Arthur came out from under a cart, dusted himself down, and held up a freshly plucked goose. 'I'm sure Sir Tate won't miss this.'

On the way back I asked why Pieshop had never mentioned that his son had joined up as well. Pieshop said that it was not what he wanted for his boy.

'He's having to work hard while he's young because I never did. I was always letting time fall through my fingers like dirt. I don't want my son to repeat the same mistakes as me.'

'Working in a knights stable is a pretty cushty job,' I said. 'He shouldn't run into any trouble.'
Pieshop gave a sad smile. 'I want him to be everything I wasn't. I want him to have every chance that I never had. I did all I could to make life better for him. And what happens, it turns out the idiot did what I did and joins the bloody army.' He said no more as we walked past the rows of battle flags.

Since arriving in Winchester, everything was moving towards war. If a spy wanted to get a message to Paris it would take a day to get to get to the coast, two days on a ship, and a days riding. If the King of France relented and wished to hand back the land, that would take another week to get back to King henry. But the timetable for war continued no matter what. We all knew we would be going to Southampton. I had not thought about dying, I held the view that I was too young for God to worry about.

   Back at the camp, they were all pleased that Pieshop's son had joined up and thought that a stable boy was a good job. But Pieshop was not so sure.

Chapter 13

I am just going outside and I may be some time
    Captain Oates

One evening, I was requested by Dr Culpepper to help deal with a patient who was having headaches. I hoped it wasn't Sir Tate. I had already made up my mind he was a bully. Along with Lord Farquar, I was beginning to get a list of enemies longer than an elephant's wang. I made up a mixture of rosemary and wormwood while Rebekah boiled up a pot of vinegar. She placed a cloth into it, and we went to the castle. At the top was a door with two guards outside. I had a small knife, which they took off me, then let us enter.

King Henry was talking with a group of other men. When he saw Rebekah, he went over to a chair. She placed the cloth soaked in warm vinegar on his forehead, he glanced at me.

'Have we met before?'

'Yes, your majesty, at the tower, of London, I was an apprentice to Sir Jeffrey Bernard.'

Henry remembered. 'Ah yes, you were either the hero who saved a damsel in distress by fighting off a lion with his bare hands, or the fool who opened the wrong door.' King Henry called to the rest of the men sat around the table. 'You see, my lords, living proof that England can take a boy at the very bottom of the pile, and turn him into someone fit to enter this room.' He looked at me. 'What are you doing in the army?'

'Dealing with piss pots, your majesty.' I said this while the smell of warm vinegar filled the room. One of the knights laughed. 'I'm now an apprentice to Doctor Culpepper,' I added.

'Aah, a noble practice,' said the King. He rubbed the scar on his face. 'I owe my life to a physician.'
I got the mixture ready. The King had an idea. 'What if I were to offer you an easier life. I need messengers to ride between Southampton, Winchester, and London. It would mean leaving your unit and missing the battle. Would you like to do it?'

'No, your majesty, I would not.'
The King laughed. 'And pray tell why?'
Rebekah moved the warm cloth. I placed the mixture of herbs on the king's forehead, taking a good look at the scar. Henry had gone into battle at the age of sixteen. He was hit in the face by an arrow. It was only stopped by his skull. He was willing to die for his country, I wanted to live because I was in love with an ordinary woman. In my silence the King found his own answer.

'Don't worry, I think I know.'
I glanced at Rebekah. The King continued. You see gentlemen, to be willing to die for one's country is a just and worthwhile thing. This man wants to die in battle with his brothers.'
I continued to apply the ointment. Luckily the King had his eyes closed. If I blushed it was only me that knew. I stopped as one of the men grabbed Rebekah and pulled her close.

'I too have something that needs easing.' He said as he squeezed Rebekah's bottom. She tried to move away. He noticed me staring. 'You, boy, when you're done here, go empty my piss pot for me. And if you spill any, I shall make you drink the rest.' He grabbed Rebekah's arm. 'And you. You look like you might have something for my groin strain. I want you waiting in my chamber when I get back.'

I told the king I would be back within the hour to take the mixture off. I left with Rebekah.

'Who was that pestilent shit house?'

'The Baron Henry Scrope,' said Rebekah. 'What am I going to do?'

'Tell him you've got the pox,' I replied.

'That doesn't say much for you.'

We walked through the castle until we saw his banner above a door. I had to think of something to save her. There was a guard standing nearby. Rebekah held up the bowl.

'Your Baron has requested his medicinal unction back,' she told him.

'What's it for?' He asked as he dipped his finger in the bowl and tasted it.

'Open pus sores on his foreskin,' Rebekah replied.

The guard spat out whatever was in his mouth and looked at me. 'Why are you here?'

'I've come to empty the piss pot.'

He opened the door. 'Be quick about yourselves, the baron is a hard taskmaster.'

I didn't know what I was looking for. Something to cause a distraction. I noticed what I first thought was a letter to a group of merchants. I read a few more lines. It was a warrant against the King. He was to be arrested...Lord Mortimer was to take his place...I read a few more lines...This was treason. I only stopped reading when I realised Rebekah was grabbing my arm.

'Come with me if you want to live.' We walked quickly towards the door. The guard outside stopped us.

'What happened to emptying the piss pot?'

I panicked. 'I drank it,' was my reply.

The guard choked slightly. He seemed happy that nothing had been stolen and let us leave.

Once outside, Rebekah looked behind to see if we were being followed.

'The baron will come looking for us, and we will both be punished. If we run away now, we might have a chance to escape.'

I stopped her.

'No.' This was my moment to prove I was a man. This was the time the Gods had chosen for me to shine.

Rebekah looked at me with those big eyes and said, 'Are you fucking mental? When Sir Scrope finds me missing he will put us in prison. You need to knock on the next door you see and ask if Sir Ronnie Reality is at home because you've lost the plot.'

I told Rebekah what I had seen. If she wanted to escape, I would not stop her. But I had a duty to tell the King, no matter what the consequences were. She thought for a moment, then had a different idea.

Chapter 14

The huntsman, he can't hunt the fox
Nor so loudly to blow his horn
And the tinker he can't mend kettle nor pot
Without a little Barleycorn
  Traffic, John Barleycorn (Must Die)

I had no idea who else was involved in this plot. Was it all the knights, every guard in the castle, was someone following us? We ran through the streets of Winchester until we reached camp. I told Rebekah to wait behind the trees. My friends were drinking and laughing around a fire. Tony had cooked a late-night snack. Derryck was leaning back against a tree.

'That's the best bucket of hedgehog I've had in ages. You can't beat a bit of greasy food after a few drinks.' He threw some broken bits of clay into the fire and looked up at me. 'We saved you the wormy one.'

I walked towards the fire. 'I need your help. Some knights are plotting to kill the King,' I said. 'If I'm right, we could die. If I'm wrong, we could die.' I explained what I had seen.

I had no idea how my friends were going to react. Perhaps they would tell me to run with Rebekah and hide in the country. As the wood in the fire crackled, Pieshop slowly stood up.

'Let me get my sword.'

Tony damped down the fire, Derryck closed the tent, Vic sharpened his dagger, Pieshop collected his sword, Arthur came out from under a cart, Icky stared at Rebekah's nipples, I picked up my longbow and some arrows, Pieshop told me to put them away. 'As far as they know, you are just an apprentice physician. I will come with you. Arthur, you go to the back of the castle and tell them you've come to sort out an emergency toothache. Vic, you follow behind him and say that you've come to play some music.'

Pieshop looked at Rebekah and then back at me. 'And if it all starts going pear shaped before we get to the King, just make sure you two can run. Get away from here, and don't look back.'

At the castle gates the guards did not seem too bothered with me or Rebekah, but Pieshop was a big man. To get in he would need a big story.

'I'm on a mission from God,' he told the guard. 'The King wishes to see the Halliwell Manuscript, for personal enlightenment.'

'Show it to me,' said a guard.

'No.'

It was a simple request, and Pieshop gave a simple answer. I thought we were meant to be trying to get into the castle as inconspicuously as possible. Now other guards were looking over. The guard asked again and got the same reply. The sheriff of Winchester joined the conversation.

'Let me see the Halliwell Manuscript.' He held out his hand. Pieshop took out Icky's dirty book. 'I shall have to tell the King you have looked.' He handed it over. 'If you refuse to give it back.'

The sheriff glanced at a few pages. 'Reminds me of that actor chap. The Bishop of Bath and Wells has something similar.' He turned. 'Let them through to see the King.'

The three of us went into the castle.

I went first up the circular steps first, followed by Rebekah, and then Pieshop. I had no idea who would be waiting for us at the top. The biggest danger would be running into Baron

Scrope. The two guards on the door recognised me and Rebekah. Pieshop was a different story. They let us in while he told them about the Halliwell Manuscript. The King was sat with two other men. His face was clean, although the scowl was not welcoming.

'Where have you been?
'Your majesty,' I said. 'I have important news.'
Pieshop came in.
'He's my friend,' I said.
The King picked up his sword then let him enter.

Once the door was closed, I told the King about the letter I had seen in Baron Scrope's room. The King asked me several questions, many of which I could not answer. My only grace was telling him I was willing to be put on trial to confirm what I had seen. Henry called for a messenger. He ordered them to fetch the sheriff, for the earl of Langley to be found and brought to him at once, and that the duke of York and Sir Thomas Erpingham be advised to attend post haste. When the messenger had gone, the King placed a hand on Pieshop's shoulder and asked if he wanted to be a royal bodyguard. To his surprise, Pieshop refused. He said he had taken an oath to protect the King and his country, but he had another code: any friend who was willing to stand by him in times of diversity would be his brother, and Pieshop was going to stay with his friends until the battle was over. King Henry looked at me.

'Perhaps I should join your band of brothers, those at the very bottom seem more willing to protect England than those at the top.'

He went over to a large velum map laid out on the table.
'How strange,' he said. 'That it should come to this.'
He turned and told me and Rebekah to hide for a few days. If there was no proof he still wanted the trial to be fair, with me giving evidence. What he didn't want was me killed.

We ran down the back steps. In the rear courtyard Arthur was nowhere to be found.

'Pssst.' Arthur came out from under a cart. He dusted himself down and walked us past Vic waiting in the wings, and led us away from the castle. Rather than back to the camp, we headed deeper into the town. The old fox seemed to know every ditch and alleyway already. He soon found what he was looking for. The circus.

Reginald Kincaid was enjoying the company of the largest prostitute I had ever seen. The cart smelled of wine, fart, sex, and sweat, the nectar of all true thespians. It was also very cramped. The prostitutes rear seemed to touch every side of the cart. Kincaid gave me a wink. You can always haggle, and they don't laugh, he said to me, as if I should be writing these words of wisdom down. He sneezed, then tried to wipe his nose with a merkin.

It was agreed we could hide for the next few days with the circus. Rebekah would pretend to be a boy pretending to be a female character in the drama group. Her real breasts would have to be covered up with false breasts. I would be one of the jesters that baited the bear.

We spent the next day watching out for any of Baron Scrope's spies. In the evening Pieshop and his son joined us, then the others arrived. There was no news yet. Rebekah was going to take part in a production of *The Millers Tale*, as a buxom wench. Although ideally suited to the role, Vic put ash on her chin and upper lip to make it appear she hadn't shaved. Icky took the false breasts…and disappeared into the bushes with them. Rebekah would just have to pretend to be a sixteen-year-old boy with real breasts playing a young wench with fake breasts.

Icky and I waited in the bear baiting tent. We watched the bear pace around its cage.

'Why does it keep walking around in circles?' Icky asked the owner.

A man with a pike staff shrugged. 'Fucked if I know.'

'Do you think it's because he's homesick?' Icky asked.

The man shook his head. 'I doubt it. He was born in a cage. He knows nothing about the forests of Transylvania.'

'But what if he just senses it,' Icky replied. 'What if he just knows there's something better than this?'

The man laughed. 'It's a dumb arsed animal. As long as its fed and entertained, its happy. So, what if it gets kicked every now and again; everybody takes a beating sometime. These thick creatures don't know anything different.'

Icky watched the bear continue to pace in a circle. 'I still think it knows there's something better than this. Maybe not better, but something more real than a cage in a circus.'

The man poked the bear. 'Every so often I take him outside and let him see the sunshine. He's frightened of his own shadow.'

Derryck came into the Marquee. There was good news. Edmund Mortimer, the Earl of March, had confessed that the plot to overthrow the King was real. Those involved had been arrested, including Baron Scrope. It was safe to go back, although we were not to speak of the matter to anyone until the trial was over.

I went to find Rebekah. She was performing on stage. There certainly seemed a lot more men than usual in the audience. Of all the feelings I had in the last twenty-four hours, fear, desperation, elation, the newest one was jealousy. When an actor kissed Rebekah and the crowd cheered, I felt my heart twist. She said later that the actor was not impressed when he found out that she was a woman pretending to be man pretending to be a woman, as he preferred the Greek method of acting.

The next morning there were new orders. The King wanted to get to Southampton to check on the ships and put the traitors on trial. No doubt all this would get back to the French Court. We spoke of how we were going to cross the sea. Few of us had ever been on a big ship. There was talk of monsters in the deep, of waves taller than a clock tower, of being lured overboard by mermaids, which were half woman, half fish.

'How does that work?' Icky asked. 'It doesn't make sense.'

'Nor does an elephant,' Derryck replied. 'But they're real.' Icky did not agree. 'An elephant has the largest penis in the world; but a mermaid either has the top half of fish lips, or the bottom half is a fin. You are pretty much going to have to sort yourself out.'

Vic joined in. 'Well done, Icky. After all this time, I think you've finally got the hand of the Socratic method.'

Icky opened out his fingers. 'Thanks. We call it something else in Liverpool. I've been doing it since I was thirteen.'

We began to move. There must have been ten thousand of us. Knights, cavalry, soldiers, archers. Add to this all the other units and the line must have stretched out for over three miles.

We arrived in Southampton to the cheers of the locals. Many of them trying to sell us something. Frothy ale, farty food, faulty feathers, and foamy fanny, seemed to be the big winners in this part of the country. There were medals of Saint Christopher for us to wear when we crossed the channel, and a list of burial prayers to put around your neck. It seemed this place catered for every part of God's plans. But something else happened before we were finally able to set sail.

Chapter 15

In default of any other proof, the thumb would convince me of the existence of a God.
   Isaac Newton.

Within the space of a few hours Southampton became a garrison town. Nearly ten thousand people were waiting to sail. The knights took the high ground. The foot soldiers were easily identified by their blue and red tunics. They tended to stay together, drinking and eating by themselves, spending time in the upmarket brothels. The archers were a bit wilder. Most wore banded kettle helmets, wearing them in the street as if they were already at work. Some had funny accents. They were going to explore Southampton whether they were allowed to or not. I thought my friends could drink, but some of these guys would do twenty pints of ale a day.

The market stalls were filled with food and weapons. I wanted to spend what savings I had buying Rebekah a new dress, but she refused, saying it would get ruined in France and that we should wait until we get back to St. Albans. This small comment cheered me greatly. It gave me hope that she saw a future with us together.

We got a bit of extra money by Arthur doing much work as a barber. Everyone wanted their hair cut very short before they left, except for me. Rebekah said she liked it long, and so I stayed looking like a boy among men.

The generals decided we needed what they called "War Games", where we would practice a battle to work out tactics. It was little Lord Farquar who rode up to our tent and explained the plan.

'Aah, my merry band of bastards. I have good news. You are on manoeuvres with the cavalry today, and I've offered you lot to play the part of the French army.'

Derryck looked around at the others. 'I think there's a few more of them than just us, sir.'

Lord Farquar was clearly enjoying himself. 'You will be joined by all the other deranged dregs from the dung bucket of society. You know the type; working class white spawn from a piss filled pond who will make no difference to England's future should they get seriously injured.'

'Does that mean you will be joining us sir,' Derryck asked. 'What I mean is, as part of the cavalry?'

Farquar shook his head. 'I shall be watching the charge with the King. I just hope there will be no injuries.'

Derryck held up his shovel. 'Oh, I think we will be alright sir.'

'I was talking about the horses; you little pig fart.' Farquar turned and looked at me. 'Not like opening a lions cage though, is it boy?'

As he left, I heard Farquar call out to his servants to find his new red bejewelled Russian codpiece and red hat with the speckled feather, as they appeared to have lost them.

'I want to put rabbit shit in his salad,' said Tony as he got the food ready.

Arthur came out from under a cart holding a red hat and suspicious bulge in his pants.

After a breakfast of smoked kippers (I avoided the salad), we were led to the middle of a field which was going to be the site of the French battle. Icky was amazed at how much it looked like England. We were ordered to stand in a thin rectangular shape along with a hundred or so other men and boys. Farquar made sure we were at the front and told everyone to wave and shout when the charge started.

Pieshop's son had sneaked into the crowd without permission just so he could see his father. We then had a smiling Pieshop tell us how big and strong his son was, how the boy could read and write his own name, that he could ride a horse, and how the girls all liked him because he took after his dad. The only moment of sadness was when Pieshop's son mentioned that Sir Tate was always slapping him every day for some minor infraction. But he did it to everyone, so it was normal. All of us, whether man or boy, who stood in that field could recount stories of being beaten by our so-called masters. Some carried scars that were worse than others, some even kept secret wounds that would never heal. We knew we were slaves to a system that would be almost impossible to change. We had not been conquered by an invading army; we simply had the misfortune to be born common.

We stopped when the drummers began to play. The cavalry to assemble at the far end of the fields. The Knights seemed more interested in their armour than listening to the Duke of York explain the tactics.

'What manoeuvre do you think they will do?' I asked Pieshop.

'It doesn't matter,' he replied. 'This is to get the horses used to charging at men. They don't want them to pull up by themselves.'

'That's the plan?'
Pieshop nodded. 'Don't forget, no plan ever survives first contact. Some of these horses are not going to stop.'

The drum roll changed to a new beat. The trumpets blew. The banners in the distance changed. We waited. The lines of horses became fluid. They came in colours, like a rainbow, while silver backed knights sat motionless riding towards us. I heard hooves hitting the earth as a thousand horses came towards us. The ground shook as if Jericho itself was falling.

'Be careful of Sir Tate' said Pieshop's son as he pointed out the knight on a large chestnut stallion. 'He wants to show the King how brave he is by knocking out those along the front line.'

We had pieces of wood, the Knights had real swords and battle axes. Pieshop moved his son behind him.

The cavalry turned in a wide arc so that the charge came from our left. The knights had to dig their spurs in to keep the horses moving forward. Three hundred yards. We were ordered to start shouting and waving. Two hundred yards. The knights on horseback must have been twelve feet off the ground. A hundred and fifty yards. I wondered if they would ever stop. The knights withdrew their swords. Now they would have to rely on one hand and their spurs to control the charging horses. The thundering of hooves grew louder. A hundred yards. Some of the horses tried to bolt, but had no room to turn or stop. The knights dug their spurs in harder. I could feel everyone around me tighten up. Fifty yards. Many of the knights in front slowed before they reached us and began to turn. Some of the horses stopped short. Others swooped around to attack at an angle.

Sir Michael Tate continued charging. He turned his horse into the line and swung his chain mace on the heads of unsuspecting targets. One old man fell to the ground, blood pouring through his fingers. We were not impressed. Sir Tate only stopped to see if the King was watching.

'What a piece of shit,' said Icky. He grabbed Tony's arm. 'Wobble,' said Icky. 'Wobble Tony as if your life depended on it.

Tony stepped out in front of the horse and wobbled wildly, waving his arms as if possessed by a windmill.

'Get out of my way, you bloody lunatic.' Sir Tate tried moving the horse.

Arthur handed Pieshop's son a speckled red hat and told the boy to cover his head with it. The boy stepped out and calmed the horse. Arthur tapped Sir Tate on the leg.

'He's raving sir,' said Arthur. 'I'm afraid the good lord has farted in the face of diversity and given this man an ill wind that makes him do the dance of Diabolos whenever the religious fervour takes over.' Arthur glanced at Icky feeding the horse and kept hold of Sir Andrews leg. 'But please don't hurt him sir, the poor man's been afflicted by a saint's curse, that's why we call him Rigalaroni Tony. This is Saint Vitus Dance sir. If you could spare just a few pennies to give to the church to help this poor man's affliction, we would be most humbly grateful.'

'Piss off, and take the jive monkey with you.'

Icky finished feeding the horse, Pieshop's son let go of the reins, Tony jiggled back into the crowd, and Arthur let go of the knight's leg.

'Thank you, sir. You knights are the best, sir.'

Sir Michael Tate kicked Arthur away and looked over at the man who had a head injury.

'You, the shirker, get up. It's just a flesh wound, get back into position.' Sir Tate rode away without looking back.

'What did you give the horse?' Derryck asked.

'Bit of sugar beet,' said Icky, 'Mixed with hemp, some fly agaric mushroom, and a few other special ingredients from my wrinkly bag; nothing serious, just something to make him ride a bit harder.'

The trumpets blew again, the drums tapped the retreat, the knights went back to their original positions to discuss tactics. Sir Tate went over to the Duke of York and demanded the next attack to be a series of direct assaults. With the King watching, the most reckless knights jostled among each other to go first.

Sir Michael Tate, and certainly his horse, chomped on the bit to get into position. The banners were raised again. The drummers erected their sticks; the trumpeters wet their lips and got ready to blow.

Without warning, Sir Tate and his horse bolted forward, jerking angrily at first, then gaining rhythm as it moved harder and faster. The trumpets and the drummers waited. Sir Tate dug his spurs in but to no avail. We watched the horse coming.

'Brace yourselves,' said Derryck.

The horse suddenly stopped. Its majestic head glistened with sweat. It bucked and jolted, then galloped around in circles as Sir Tate shouted and beat his hand upon the animals back. The King was not amused. Lord Farquar was ordered to go down and see what was happening. He rode over to Sir Tate and told him to get back into line. The horse, noticing the brood mare that Farquar sat astride on, became very aroused.

'Jesus,' said Arthur. 'It's like an elephant's penis.'

'More like a giants thumb,' Vic replied. 'Look at the way it moves, almost able to bend at will.'

Lord Farquar jumped down from his horse to remonstrate, but Sir Tate was not quick enough to dismount from his own. His stallion raised itself up and rogered its conquest to the cheers of everyone. The poor bastard must have been waiting years to get some. Farquar tried to pull his mare away, but she seemed happy to let nature take its course. Sir Tate tried slapping the hind legs but it only seemed to encourage his stallion. Arthur reckoned it was now going fast enough to win the 3.30 at Kempston. Eventually the mare bolted forward. As it did so, the stallion, in a mighty drug induced rapture, shot its magnificent load directly into the face of little Lord Farquar.

'Bullseye,' said Tony, and gave a little jiggle.

Icky, whose imagination revolved around food and sex, could only shake his head. 'That's put me right off the rice pudding I was going to have for me scran.'

Sir Tate waited for his horse to become flaccid. His face was also an enraged red. He pointed his sword at Farquar.

'You sir. Who the hell are you?'

Farquar wiped his eyes clean. 'Me sir. I am Lord Norman Farquar, from the Littlehampton Farquars. I'll have you know I am related to the royal family, on my mother's side.'

Sir Tate lowered his sword. 'Aah, so you're one of those little mother Farquar's I've heard about. I shall be speaking to the King about this matter.' The angry Sir Tate and his happy horse limped off the field of play.

Farquar turned and saw his red hat on the ground.

'That's my hat. Who stole it? He looked through the crowd and saw me. 'You. I bet you had a hand in this. I'm going to wipe the smile off your face boy, I'm going to make you swallow your pride, and then I am going to make sure you are bloody well hung.'

It was difficult to take him seriously due to a large white globule hanging from the tip of his nose. Farquar stopped as the King and his guards rode up.

'This was deliberate,' Farquar said, covered in Lady Godiva's shampoo. 'One man in that mob instigated this mess to try and start an uprising.'

'Did you know who it is?' The King asked him.

Farquar looked again at me, but after the previous trial, could only shake his head. 'I cannot prove if it was a boy, but I'll be blowed if I am going to let them leave here with egg on my face.'

All one hundred of us were ordered to sit down by the King. As the great ancient poets and military historians used to say, shit had just got real. We were the bottom of society. Anyone accused of disobeying a military order would be arrested for treason. In the current climate the King could have us killed on the spot. We waited to see what his wrath would be.

He rode along the front line, staring at each of us in turn, close enough for each man and boy to see the large scar on his face where he had taken an arrow for his country. He was a warrior, while we had been larking around like kids. He shouted loud enough for those at the back to hear.

'Men of England. Serfs you were, and serfs you remain. Even though we are on the eve of war, there are knights in prison because they tried to stop my destiny. They forgot that I am on a mission from God. And God will not let me fail here in a field of cow shit and horse cunk.' He turned and trotted back across the front line. 'I promise you I am a just leader. Lord Farquar has informed me that someone among you has committed an insurrection. I do not know if that is true. But if foul play was involved, you need to name the man. That individual will be punished as per military rules. Or this whole group can stand in this field until we leave for France.' He stopped his horse. 'What say you men of England. Is there anyone among you willing to be punished to save the others?'

There was silence. The King waited. Men sat in the field as the flies buzzed around them. The Kings guards drew their swords. Sir Michael Tate rode back down. If he recognised Pieshop's son there would be trouble.

'What say you men of England,' the King asked. 'Are you all prepared to be punished rather than see one man take the blame?'

Pieshop's son's hands were shaking. Pieshop went to stand up. Deryck placed a hand on his friends' shoulder and pushed him back down. He stood up in front of a defeated army and called out to the King.

'I'm Spartacus.'

There was silence in the field. Men looked around at each other. Icky stood up. 'I'm Spartacus.'
Tony stood up next to his friend. 'I'm Spartacus.'
Vic stood up and pointed at Arthur. 'I'm Spartacus and so is my dad.'
Other men began to stand up and call out that they were Spartacus. I stood up. Pieshop held on to his son and smiled as everyone around him also stood up and declared themselves to be Spartacus. We stand alone together. I saw the King smiling. He held up his hand, bade us all safe journey and called over to his generals.

'I would rather go into battle with this band of bastards, than the richest knights who only seek glory for themselves.'
He then turned back to us. 'A drink on me for every man here.' The men cheered, more for the promise of free booze than anything else. I noticed that the generals had rolled up their plans and put them away. So far, we had merely played at being soldiers. The time for real fighting would soon begin.

Chapter 16

We're the masters of our own fate
The painter and the paint
　Robbie Williams, Forbidden Road.

We were getting ready to sail. There was no sign of the French handing back the land they had taken. How much time we had left, I did not know, but we were ordered to make ready. Sup up your beer and collect your fags, so it would be easier to start a fire when we got there.

　Only Pieshop and Vic had been on a ship. Arthur, England's oldest Viking, said the sea air was not good for his cough. His last journey over water was on a pedalo. I had heard stories of waves as high as church towers, sailors going mad with thirst, man-eating monsters that lurked in the deep, and ships that had simply disappeared in the mist. The people around here seemed to spend more time talking about the sea than being on it. We decided to have a jolly boys outing to take our minds off it. Rebekah came with us to collect bundles of Yarrow.

　My first sight of the sea was at it lay on the horizon. It looked higher than the land. On the beach I watched the waves break over the sand. Vic told us that the ancient Greeks believed the tide was connected to the moon, that's why no one sailed at night.

　'If the world is round, why doesn't all the water fall off?' Rebekah asked. Vic picked up a bucket with a length of rope on the handle. He partly filled it with water, then took the small hourglass from his jacket.

'Imagine we are grains of sand in this hourglass. If I place it in the water and keep it turning around, our lives still move in the time it takes to get from the top of the hourglass to the bottom. But what if the world is spinning as well?' He held the rope and spun the bucket around. 'Even when the bucket reaches the top and the water is upside down, it does not fall out. And we never notice, living in our little hourglass, each grain of sand marking the passage of time.'

I was not so sure. 'I thought you said time was a flat circle. How can time be flat, and the world be round?'

'What if everything around us is spinning as well,' Vic replied. 'This world, the stars, and even history. What if everything we've done has been done before in a slightly different way, and will do again at some point in the future. Just as this bucket spins, and the hourglass spins inside it, no grain of sand will ever land next to the one it did before. But it's always the same sand. Time keeps moving, turning inside this inner world with every spin of an outer world as it swings around like a carousel. For every empire that has gone, a new one will rise and die. Perhaps you have the same hopes and dreams as your father Harry, probably saying at some point that you will never be like him, only to grow old and find out you are.'

The last bit caught me in the stomach. 'Is that true?'

Vic put the bucket down.

'Not exactly the same. The greater our knowledge, the more chance we have of breaking free from our own past. But the past never really ends. We walk among the ancestors of those who walked in the footsteps of Jesus.'

I watched the waves roll in with youthful noise before they slowly faded back out back out. In truth I still felt the pain of my father's death and the worry that I would be doomed to repeat the same thing.

We walked into Southampton. The plan was to find a tavern. And then we saw the port. I have seen the docks of London crowded with boats from all over the world. Here in Southampton, there were a thousand ships. I remembered something in the Bible about the *Lust of the Eye*. Now I knew what it meant. War, in all its horror, was also a thing of terrible beauty. Hannibal had elephants; King Henry had warships. Using these mammoth machines, we were about to embark upon the great crusade toward which we had striven these many months. We all felt something stir within us. Pieshop made the sign of the cross. Arthur, Icky, and Tony went to a local knocking shop.

The rest of us waited in the downstairs part of a tavern. Arthur came back first.

'I had the fat one,' he said, then ordered the Stargazy pie to get his strength back.

As he ate, Pieshop's' son came in to say he had been looking everywhere for us. The Southampton plotters had just confessed to try and dethrone the king. They would be executed tomorrow at dawn. It also meant their ranks needed to be filled. Lord Farquar had been promoted to General. This was good news for us, as it meant we would not have to see him again. Only Pieshop was unhappy. A poor leader is not someone who makes bad decisions, its someone who makes no decisions. Farquar in charge of a frontline unit would lead to many mistakes, and many deaths. But there was more.

Little Lord Fuckpants did not want to go into battle. Pieshop's son had heard Farquar had paid a group of stable boys to attack him tonight, enough to put him in an infirmary until after the army had left.

When Icky and Tony came down, Icky gave me the thumbs up.

'Smell it,' he said. 'Always worth paying extra for that; no offence Rebekah.'

We told them of the situation. A plan was suggested. If caught, we could all be hung. It didn't matter. We were a team. We all agreed. Norman Farquar was as incompetent as he was arrogant. Letting him loose on a battlefield would mean many men would end up dead. If he wanted to stay here, then so be it. But it would be on our terms.

Later that night a freshly cleaned Farquar made a point of showing the landlord of a local tavern a gold coin as he asked for one small glass of wine, and the change. A short time later he came out of the tavern shaking his pouch and headed towards the port. He had planned for the robbery to take place behind Holyrood Church, where no doubt a justice of the peace would eventually find him and call for help. The hardest thing would be to avoid the prostitutes hanging around. Part of his original idea was for one of the stable boys to dress up as a woman so they could walk down an alleyway without anyone finding it strange. We met Smollet, paid him his money, and told him to leave.

Rebekah was given a false moustache from Reginald Kincaid, who was waiting around the corner. He said the way to attract Farquar's attention was for her to gently stroke her hairy lips. Farquar, believing it was Smollet, joined her. Once they reached the darkest corner, Farquar prepared himself.

'Try not to hit the face. It's still a bit salty.' A sack was quickly put over his head. 'Good idea,' he said, not sure if it was his own idea.

Rebekah punched him in the stomach, which dropped Farquar to the floor. Pieshop picked him back up and we all got a few punches in. Icky then produced an enormously large black leather truncheon, weighted at one end with two orbs, and gave Farquar a good pummelling.

'Is that you mother?' Farquar asked.

'Take his pantaloons off,' said Icky as he rested the orbs on top of Farquar's head. 'Let him plead. Adds a bit of spice.'

'No, really,' Farquar said from inside his sack. 'You've all done a smashing job. I think I've got enough now to stay here rather than fight. Let the working-class scumbags do that, eh.' Icky hit Farquar in the face with the python of love, and Rebekah knocked Farquar out with one punch.

Rebekah changed into the dukes' clothes, and Farquar was put into the dress. His parents should have given Norman Farquar the name of William, like the conqueror, or little Willy for short. We placed the unconscious Farquar into the back of Kincaid's cart and it rattled away into the night. Arthur climbed out from under a bench and dusted himself down. Somehow, he had managed to take all of Farquar's jewellery and coins without any of us noticing. He shared out the money.
Icky waved the black love carrot of Diabolos. 'I shall be thinking about those bangers all night. Thanks Becky.'
Rebekah gave him the thumbs up. She knew she had great knockers.

The plan was for Kincaid to drop Farquar off at a rest home for mildly interesting sailors. By the time he managed to convince someone of who he is, we would have already sailed. Which means a real general will take his place. With this one act we may have even just won the war against France.
We went to the local tavern to celebrate. The landlord told us that Kincaid had drunk seven bottles of wine that night and left without paying the bill. We paid in full, and still had enough to get roaring drunk.

The next morning, we were ordered down to port. The first ships were already on the horizon. The invasion was really happening. I think all of us said a prayer at that moment. We were told we would be on the last set of ships to leave. Good. I felt as rough as a badgers arse. One mad woman stopped me.

'Beware the one-eyed lesbian of Little Hampton,' she said. 'No man has survived her growler.'

'Doe sit bite?' I asked, not knowing what she was talking about.

'I wouldn't wave your finger at it,' she replied.

I thanked her for the advice. As I slowly walked along the port an old sailor called over at me.

'Sea-sick?'

I looked down on the floor, 'where?' At this point I was hit on the side of the head by a wooden beam. I woke up being held by the old man and the mad woman. To clear my head, I stood and watched the ripples change their size. Was every wave different every single time? I felt seasick even though I was still on dry land. Rebekah would be getting on her own ship. As a nurse she would be treated like a nun by the English army. How she would be treated if captured by the French, I didn't know. I thanked the people and walked towards my ship.

For the next few days, we would be nothing but grains of sand being tossed around in a big wooden bucket. I was at the mercy of every known and unknown forces in the universe. How quickly I had gone from the glass cage of boyhood to a world turned upside down with every wave. Everything spun around, going up and down, up and down…I reached the sick bucket just in time.

Chapter 17

"A dry martini," Bond said. "One. In a deep champagne goblet."
"Oui, monsieur."
"Just a moment. Three measures of Gordon's, one of vodka, half a measure of Kina Lillet. Shake it very well until it's ice-cold, then add a large thin slice of lemon peel. Got it?"
"Certainly, monsieur."
   Ian Fleming, Casino Royal.

We boarded on the 11th of August 1415. Our ship was the *Decameron*. The name came from a book about a group of travellers telling stories. But the word was older than that. Dr Culpepper told me it originated from the Greek word for ten, the most important number in their system, as it allowed them to map out the distances between each island. I was sailing on a ship made up of words. I was a Cantonaut (at least that's what I think an old sailor called me). Ten thousand men sailing into the unknown, and I was just a tiny part of it.

The top deck was filled with Knights, rich physicians, and men from the Kings privy council. The lower deck had various men from the ministry. We were underneath them, next to a bilge pipe. The stern had been taken over by an exclusive coterie of high-class whores. They were run by the redoubtable Ophelia MacCracken, who offered a selection of services to her wealthy clients. When she saw my long hair and young face, she smiled.

'Always happy to give a special price for virgin soldiers.'

'He's not,' said Derryck.

'Not what?'

'A soldier.' Derryck smiled. 'He had a bit of a ding dong with our boss, so we got put on permanent latrine duty.'

Miss MacCracken smiled. 'They say an army marches on its stomach; that must be why so many generals are full of piss and wind. I am Ophelia MacCracken,' she said, 'But you can call me Phil.' She and Derryck took an instant liking to each other, as they saw everything through the lens of money. 'Are you a naval man Derryck?'

Derryck finished his pot of jellied eels. 'Well, my dear old nan always used to say I came from a long line of sea men. But once I've done my bit for England I intend to settle down, with the right woman, of course. Are you going to stay in the sex business, Phil MacCracken?'

She shook her head. 'Once this is over, I plan to go back home and take a break from work, spend some time standing up.'

'There's such a romantic dulcet tone in your voice,' said Derryck. 'Are you from some faraway island demi- paradise kissed by the sun?'

She raised her glass. 'Close. Its above knocking shop just off the Balls Pond Road.'

I left them to it.

Tony was the only one smiling. He finally felt normal. While everyone else was rolling and hitting the beams, he somehow seemed to be as steady as a rock. Whenever a wave hit, he would shout 'Rollocks' at the top of his voice. Having been brought up in a meat market, the smell of someone heaving their guts didn't bother him. Icky gave me some hemp cake to help ease the big lump on the side of my head. After a while it made me feel like a melted candle. Arthur handed me a bottle wine to give me sea legs.

I told Dr Culpepper about hitting my head. He gave me a pouch of poppy seeds and a manuscript by the Greek surgeon Galen to read. After I poured myself another pint I got into the book. The images of the human body on the page reminded me of a ship. Limbs were masts, the brain was the captain, skin was the sails. The hull became a skeleton and the organs were various cabins. I thought maybe the sailors were the blood of the ship, keeping it moving, keeping it alive. I didn't know if it was the booze, the poppy seeds, the book, the hemp cake, or the waves, but I felt as if a profound insight had been handed to me. As I studied the drawings of ape skulls I knew I was a man of learning. Soon I had drunk a second bottle.

And now I must confess my head had been turned by one of Miss MacCracken's women. But in the same way a man could read a menu and not want a gobble, I felt that I could look at look at breasts with impunity. I was almost a doctor for Christs sake. She was old, perhaps thirty-five. She wore a thin white lace vest. She asked me about the book. I told her I was training to be a physician. She had been on her back all day and needed to soothe her aching bones. Even though I was an apprentice I agreed to help. That's how much I love learning.

We went into her cabin. She handed me a jar of oil, told me to massage her back and slipped out of her dress. I did the best I could. When she turned around, I could not take my eyes off her tits. Becky had great love dumplings, firm and juicy, New Testament stuff. But these were the crown jewels of knockers. Truly Biblical breasts. Full and ripe, and each one you wanted to kiss as if they were toffee apples in a fair. Her nipples were as perky as a deer's nose. Even though the hemp cake had made my mind soft, and the wine had spun me around all day, her body made my resolve quickly stiffen. She told me to rub the oil into her shoulders. She was warm, like an Egyptian cat. Her white skin glistened with the wet oil. With every press of my thumb, I felt Mr Love Sausage of Trouser town desperate to come out and say "Hello, how are you today?" I told her I had no money. She explained that doctors and priests get it for free (Halleluiah for science).

She went down on her knees. My cock bounced out like a broom handle in a badly decorated room. It is said that the act she performed on me was invented by the Egyptians to help bring their Gods to life. No wonder Moses joined them.

There was a danger point when the cabin began to spin even though my eyes were open. Perhaps she was blowing air into me? I tried to think of something else. The first thing that came into my mind were the anatomical drawings of the small monkey skulls in my medical manuscript. She stopped.

'What are you saying?'

'A little head,' I replied, still thinking of the drawings. 'Just a little head.'

Soon my legs began to buckle. I let out a moan. She finished by shivering my timber. After it was over, I thanked her (not with a kiss). Then I picked up my medical book left. After professing my love for Rebekah, you could say I was a cheat and a sinner; but I saw it more as a wonderful nightcap and a practical guide on anatomy. They need to give name to what she had just done to me. I'm surprised the Greeks didn't come first on that one.

I went up on deck to get some air. There must have been thousands of stars that night. If they were all the same as earth, was another young lad watching on a ship just like me. Perhaps there was one planet where a boy was still living with his father, another planet where the war was already over, another one where my father was still alive. Were there other planets where I had lived or died, on this ship, this country, this island earth?

The stars kept moving around and around and around. I had travelled through space and time within the relative dimensions of this earthly vessel. The morning would see me in France. As well as saving a life, I knew I may also have to take one. I leaned over the deck and threw up into the waves.

PART 3

WE APPEAR TO HAVE GONE ON HOLIDAY BY MISTAKE

Chapter 18

Are you gonna sit in some poxy office with a cunt for a boss telling you what to do as you count your pennies trying to make ends meet in a country that's sinking into strikes and wars, and at the end of the day you go home to your cosy little flat in 'nowheresville' and pull your IKEA curtains shut to hide from the big bad world and pretend it's not happening? Or are you gonna stand up and be counted, make a difference, and feel the rush? Just for once say "fuck it". I'm coiled up like a spring and I'm ready to burst and wanking ain't doing it anymore. I need violence to make me feel I'm still alive. I know what I'd rather do, mate. Tottenham away. Love it!
    FOOTBALL FACTORY.

13th August 1415. The feast day of St Hippolytus, one of the first writers on Christianity. He criticised the Pope and was punished by being dragged by horses through the streets until he was dead; so, not a good day for him. Today was also the last day of feasting for those who believed in the transfiguration, when Christ became more than just a man. The first thing I did when I woke up was check my penis. No marks or sores. I had not transformed into a pox riddled piss artist (so not a writer).

    I went up on deck to find the sailors running around in a panic. We had strayed past our landing point. The captain was happy to take counsel with the physicians. To turn the ship around and catch enough wind to go back to Harfleur would take at least another day. We looked across the sea to a beach.

    'What's that place called?' Pieshop asked.

    'Lion-sur-Mer,' the captain replied.

Pieshop smiled' 'Lion. Can you drop us off. We will start the war from here.'

The seven of us were put into a small boat. We had our shovels, packs filled with food, our longbows, a bag of arrows, Arthur's helmet, and that was pretty much it. As an extra precaution against being attacked, Vic also had his lute. Icky said we should have waited on the boat. Those prostitutes would have given us a discount in the end.

We stormed the beaches of Normandy at the rate of two men rowing as slowly as they could. Before the waves broke the sailors told us to get out. Pieshop dipped his longbow into the water and told the sailors to take us all the way to the beach, otherwise the only thing bobbing on the waves would be their balls. They rowed until we heard the sound of sand rubbing against the hull. As soon as our feet went overboard, the sailors were rowing back to the ship, fearful of meeting an angry French army.

'Never get out of the boat,' said Icky as we waded to shore. 'Never get out of the boat. How the fuck are we going to invade France?'

I looked along the horizon. We could be attacked at any moment. Never get out of the boat. Icky was absolutely goddam right; unless you were going all the way, and we were.

The sun was shining, the sea was a crystal blue, the sand a golden yellow, trees bloomed, birds glided across the sky. Derryck looked along the beach.

'What an absolute shit hole. Not one winkle stall for miles.'

I looked as well. If this was a war zone, the only casualty so far was a fish Tony had stepped on. The real English army had landed about twenty miles away, another day's march in this heat. Our plan should have been simple enough, follow the shoreline north and eventually we would reach the port of Harfleur and join the physician's unit. But even the simplest of plans will suffer when left in the hands of simple men.

'Let's go see the Bayeux Tapestry,' said Icky. 'It's not that far from here. We've got at least two days before anyone is going to miss us. We could make it a bit of a trip.'

'Not a bad idea,' said Derrick as we put our boots back on. 'Have a few drinks, see the sights, and then back in time for tea and medals.' He looked around. 'Where is this Bayeux Tapestry then?'

'In Bayeux,' said Vic.

Only Pieshop and me wanted to join the others at Harfleur. I wanted to see Rebekah, Pieshop wanted to make sure his son was safe. Derryck had arranged to meet Ophelia, but this was only after she had set up her office in a cart with good suspension. And so, after a group decision, we headed away from what was really happening in Europe and went off to see an image of our English past because Icky believed the tapestry would have naked women. Another group decision was to lose the tunics. I thought it was a bit pointless, as our longbows marked us out as English, and no doubt the French sailors had already reported the invasion.

My first impression of France was that it seemed bigger than England. There were still church towers in the distance, but the roads were not as good and I was not sure about all the plants. The trees looked the same. Variations of Oak, Elder, Elm and Ash. It also felt a bit warmer. Moving up from the beach we came to our first contact with the enemy. Three old French women sat weaving wicker baskets.

'I've got this,' said Derryck. He walked up to them. 'Au revoir.' He pointed out towards the sea. 'Je suis from Perfidious Albion. I am Deryck Dubois.' He pointed at me. 'Moi friend is Harry le Roy.' He pointed at Vic. 'This is Sir Renault Clio, and the large gentleman at the back is Booker Newberry the Third.'

'Are they your non de plumes?' asked the woman.

'I'm terribly sorry.' Derryck buttoned the front of his trousers 'I have come here to…' He saw the church tower. 'Clack your bells.'

She looked at us. 'You are campanologists?'

'Vic might be,' said Derryck. 'No, we've just come to tour your churches. In no way are we soldiers.'

'You are definitely not knights. You look like a group of English wideboys who want to visit the tapestry.'

'That's right. Here, how do you know we're not noblemen?' She smiled. 'The English are branded on their tongue.' She pointed to a path behind her. 'Take this road to Caen. Everyone knows the English army has landed; but don't worry, you will be safe.'

'Why,' said Derryck. 'Is it because they can see we're just ordinary men rather than a band of soldiers?'

'No. It's because you look like simpletons.' She replied as she stared at Arthur in his Viking helmet. 'The only thing he should be fighting is his hairline.' She looked at the clasp on the top of my longbow. 'What shell is that from?'

'An elephant,' I replied.

She came over to look. 'The pearl white reminds me of something from my youth.' Her French accent resonated like old love letters hanging on the line to dry. 'How much?'

'It's his good luck charm,' said Pieshop. He began to march. I gave the lady some of my salted pork and joined the others. She called out to us. 'If you really are interested in campanology, there is the church of Saint Marcel in the next village where you can have a little tinkle, Mr Dubois.'

'No thanks,' said Derryck. 'I had one before we got off the boat.'

She had one final thought for us all. 'Stay on the path, boys. Keep clear of the moors and beware the moon.'

The track twisted and turned under high hedgerows. The ground was dry, and the land was filled with walnut, cork, and olive orchards. After a few hours we stopped at a farm. They sold us some bread, cheese, and wine (which I avoided). I had milk, which was the best milk I have ever drank in my life. I must also confess that it was the finest bread I had ever tasted. I told the farmer's wife this, and with a big smile she remarked how good my French was.

  The children on the farm were excited to see English people. Icky showed them how to play football, then complained that they kept diving. Vic taught them a song. Pieshop carved out a sword for one boy, Arthur sat while a girl put a crown of daisy chains through his long hair and beard. They had a pond where we could swim. Afterwards we decided to take a well-earned nap to dry. War is hell…for other people. By the time we woke up the sun was on the wane. If we made Caen by nightfall we could be in Bayeux by the next morning. And if the locals were this friendly the trip should be a breeze.

Chapter 19

I'll never forget where I'm from, never forget my roots. It doesn't matter where I live. I'm English, simple as that.
   David Beckham.

As the shadows faded, we decided to pop into the nearest village café. It was a nice rustic place, painted yellow, with a wall removed for people to sit outside with their goats. The locals looked at bit gormless, which wasn't surprising as they drank wine by the pint. We soon got on it. As the sun finally set, we were as pissed as the French plumbing. I tried talking to a goat, first in English, then in French. The fucking thing understood French better than me. Icky wanted to know more about the tapestry and decided he was going to converse with the old peasants on the next table.

'What's French for touching cloth in the big house?' He asked Vic.

'Chateau Le Pants,' said Vic.

Icky turned to one old man sat at the next table. 'These French tapestries,' he said. 'Is there any, you know, nudity?'

The man consulted with his drinking partner. Their accents were so coarse it was almost impossible to keep up. The old man turned and nodded.

'I knew it,' said Icky as he rubbed his hands on his knees. 'I bet its really saucy stuff. The French are always showing off their hairy bits and calling it art. Just imagine all that flesh on a big screen.' Icky called for the landlord to bring out the finest bucket of wine known to humanity.

'What's the stitching like,' said Icky. 'Is it a bit blurry, or can you see everything? I know there's a bit about someone getting a load in the eye about halfway through, but do they start showing the dirty stuff in the first couple of scenes?'

The man drank slowly, letting a trickle of wine pour down his chin, then said in his best Anglaise.

'There are exactly ninety-three penises.'

Icky urged him on. 'What are they doing?'

'Mostly flopping about.'

'On a woman's face?'

The man shook his head. 'There are no naked women in the tapestry.'

'Hang on,' said Icky. 'Let me get my head around this. You've got ninety-three nobs knitted by nuns, but not one single fanny or pair of knockers?'

'Correct. We are French,' came the reply.

It slowly dawned on Icky that he had made a terrible mistake. 'You mean we've come all this bloody way to look at French cocks?' He stood up, swaying from side to side. 'We should have stayed on the fucking boat.' He looked down. 'Where's my kit bag?'

Both Derryck and Tony, who had been sitting with their back to the café, realised their bags had also gone. Icky started scuffling with a burly French farmer. Derryck stumbled forward.

'You thieving little mint leaves.' He grabbed the nearest Frenchman and demanded to know where his bag had gone. A buck toothed man sitting at the table put his hand into his cloak. Pieshop stepped forward and pointed at him. 'That had better be a carrot you're reaching for, because whatever you pull out, it's going in your fucking mouth.'

Icky then gave one Frenchman a scouse kiss. Derryck punched the man in front of him as men came swaggering over.

One of them grabbed me. I punched him in the stomach, and he went down like a sack of petit-pois. One of the men laughed at Tony as he jiggled slightly, and pushed him. Tony fell, killing a goat. Derryck ran over, no fear that the man was a lot bigger, and punched him. Icky, with his insatiable lust shot down by exactly ninety-three penises, put all his effort into fighting rather than fornicating. He took out two men and went to punch a large farm worker. Unfortunately, the farm worker took the punch, and threw one back. As Icky fell backwards, I remembered my training from Pieshop. I ran up, planted my feet, and threw a straight right on the jaw. Tony started swinging with his shovel. The men were not physically strong, but we were beginning to get outnumbered. I had been in France for less than a day and was about to lose everything. But something inside me found it liked the fight. I was ready for more. Then we all stopped. The men had us surrounded. Some had pitchforks, some had axes. Pieshop took out his knife. I grabbed my longbow. How this would turn out I didn't know, but we were all ready. A voice called out in the darkness.

'Monsieur's,' said Vic.

I turned to see that he was standing a short distance up the road, just behind a wall. Although it was dark, he was pointing something at the group. 'I am Vic Flange, the most famous crossbow shooter in Europe. I am feared throughout the streets of Berlin, wanted by the Borgias in Barcelona, and not to popular with the catholic school in Stoke on Trent. From here I can kill at least three of you, and make the fourth man Jewish. Return the bags, and let my friends go.'

The men knew they could beat us, but wanted to keep their balls. The kitbags were thrown to the ground. Arthur came out from under a cart and dusted himself down. He picked up his Viking helmet and took out a handful of coins from his pocket.

'Keep the change, you filthy animals.' He threw the coins down the dusty road. The French men all stood still, not sure if it was a trap.
As I looked around, I saw the name of the café, it was *La Lunaire*. Beware the moon.

We grabbed our stuff and ran up towards Vic, who told us to keep going. After a short while we heard him call out to the men that they could pick up the coins. A few moments later he caught up with us, and we kept running.

'You didn't have to throw away your money,' Vic said. Arthur shook his head. 'I never. I nicked it from the landlord's safe upstairs. Where did you get the crossbow from?'

'It was my lute,' said Vic. 'When they turned to pick up the money, I wedged it into the wall. They think I am still watching them right now.'

We kept moving through a moonlit forest. Icky needed to sit down.

'We should have never of got off the boat.'
Derryck agreed. 'Who the bleeding hell goes to another country in the middle of August to swan around getting drunk, starting fights and trying to get laid? Theres a fortune to be made out of these carrot crunchers.'

'I think its bloody brilliant,' said Tony. 'This is the best time I've ever had in my life.' He looked at me. 'It's not about the money is it Harry. It's the charge, it's the bolt, it's the buzz, it's the sheer fuck off-ness of it all. Am I right?'
I put my arm around him. Yes, he was. Truth be told, there was something about knowing you could handle yourself that gave you confidence. The army had forged a friendship where we all knew we could rely on each other.

Pieshop told us to be quiet. We ducked down as voices rose on the road. What the fuck was that? One of them had a lute, and they were singing a song that some of us knew well.

'Greensleeves était toute ma joie
Greensleeves était mon délice.'

'Aah,' said Vic. 'So that's the song you've all been talking about. It will never catch on.'

We waited for the danger to pass. With that, our first day in France had come to an end. We had fought our first battle, and the only casualty was a goat that understood French a little too well. I hoped we would be a bit wiser by the time we butted heads against the real enemy.

Chapter 20

Is there anybody going to listen to my story
All about the girl who came to stay?
She's the kind of girl you want so much it makes you sorry
Still you don't regret a single day
   The Beatles, Girl.

As we walked towards Harfleur, I told the others about what had happened on the ship. They all had a difference of opinion, like blind men touching a different part of an elephant, all wondering if it's his nob.

'Tell Rebekah the truth,' said Pieshop.

'Put your faith on modern love,' said Vic.

'Hang on,' said Icky. 'What happens on tour stays on tour, and what doesn't kill her won't hurt her. He only gave the hooker a choirboy's breakfast. I say he doesn't tell her.'

As they started to give accounts of their own adventures, I felt that Icky's was the best answer.

By the time we got to Harfleur the siege had already begun. The place was not so much a castle, more a fortified city. The main wall must have been over three miles long. One side was bordered by the river Siene, another side was bordered by the harbour and the sea. Another side looked out onto fields. The wall at the back looked out onto the road that led to Paris.

Bored French soldiers watched from the turrets. Farmers moved their cows out of the fields for the English to put their tents in. It all seemed a bit of a phoney war. Rumours abounded that as soon as Paris agreed to hand over the town to King

Henry, we could all go home; at a cost of a thousand pounds to the Kings coffers.

We put on our black tunics with the white cross and looked for the hospital camp with the emblem of two snakes wrapped around a winged staff. This gave the place an element of sanctuary. As we walked up, a big bearded armoured soldier from the Welsh brigade, stopped us.

'Hello honky tonks.

'Hello Paz,' said Derryck. 'How's tricks?'

A bolt from a crossbow flew across. We ducked slightly; Paz didn't move. 'They fire a few out every so often, pointless really.'

'Why because there are so many of us?'

Paz picked up a bolt from the ground. 'No, none of them have got any sharpened points. Some general was looking for you. There's no more space in the encampment. You'll have to go into town and find somewhere.' Another crossbow bolt flew by. It hit a tree and bounced off.

We found a run-down set of huts near the sea. The hotel was titled "Chattes Fleuries," and run by a large bossy woman.

'What a dump,' said Icky. 'This has got to be the worst hotel in the whole of Western Europe.'

'No,' said Vic. 'No, I won't have that. Theres a place in Eastbourne.'

The big brassy old woman had some sheds in the back we could use. Icky called her the Queen of the Harpies (I think). Arthur decided to claim first dibs by telling the rest of us, 'I like em curvy.' We all thought he had said "Scurvy", so didn't complain. Her name was Livia Renoir. We called her Olive; on account her teeth were pitted green and black. She may have sworn like a trooper and her belly was competing with her bottom to see who could get away from her spine first, but she was a happy old dear and I liked her.

During the day she pickled onions in the back garden, which she sold to the locals. Of an evening, she would walk out and steal wine from the vineyards. This was more of a hobby than a crime. She would have stolen more, but she suffered from uncontrollable flatulence. Even the guard dogs were sick. We promised to pay her a few shillings a week for board and food, and we dug over the part of her garden near the beach to plant sea wort. Arthur noticed her admiring his helmet and told her he was a Viking. Within three days he had his feet under the table and was plundering Olive most nights after they got back from nicking booze. In his own way Arthur believed he had opened a second front, at least that's what I think I heard him say. I would lie there in the darkness listening to her crunch pickled onions and call out 'Ooh Arthur,' as he brought his longboat into shore.

At first things went pretty well. Soldiers built wooden ballistic machines and started to dig a tunnel to breach the wall. The others agreed I could help Dr Culpepper, on the basis that the more he taught me about medicine, the more I would help them if they were injured. Sir Thomas Erpingham believed we would be home by harvest time. But I am getting slightly ahead of myself. There was the other incident which I must deal with first.

In that first week I would go to the beach with Rebekah as often as I could. I would sit with her in the moonlight. She would talk about how beautiful the sea or the sky was. I never noticed it. All I cared about was being with her. Whenever she took hold of my hand her touch was warm and feminine. I don't think I had ever been so happy. A blind man could fall in love with her just from her voice.

'They say we are just waiting for the message of surrender from Paris, and then the siege will be over. We could both be home before the harvest. I bet by then most of the knights would have caught the pox from that brothel on the far side of the camp.'

I needed to change the subject. It sounds crude, but my main thought was wondering when I was going to plough her ripe warm fields again. I knew I should confess. I wanted to tell her that I had fallen before I got on the ship, and I had not eaten a thing all day, apart from hemp cake and a bag of poppy seeds, and I was forced to drink two bottles of wine that I had never drank before, and because I had a book of monkeys one of the women thought I was a doctor, an honest mistake by a grown woman and a sixteen year old boy, and she made me treat her back. Somehow, somehow, and we will probably laugh about this in many years' time, my trousers fell down, and she plumbed my mast to the sound of snores from salty seamen, all just a total misunderstanding that we will probably have a good laugh about on our wedding day. That's what I wanted to say. Instead, I said, 'I love you.'
She squeezed my hand as if she was bursting with so much love that she had to transfer some of it to me. 'I love you to.'

I'm afraid to say I kissed her more out of ending the conversation than showing my undying love for her. I wanted to be with her for the rest of my life. I also knew I wanted some right now. We walked along the beach until we found clumps of tall sea grass. We kissed in the summer moonlight. Her breasts rested against my chest. Her warm soft buttocks folded in my hands. The smoothness of her inner thighs flexed every sinew in my body. I was with a woman who also wanted me. I silently begged for forgiveness and vowed to never be unfaithful again. I laid her down in the sand and opened her dress. I then quietly thanked Jesus.

Every kiss peeled away another layer of my soul until we had become one. We entwined our bodies in the heat of the night. Every kiss, every touch, every movement just seemed to feel right. She was simply perfection. Even with the smell of pickled onions in the air, I quickly managed to get to the vinegar strokes. Then came the loudest bang I had ever heard.

'That's a big one,' said Rebekah.

'Thank you, my mum says I get it from my dad. How was that?'

She adjusted her dress. 'You're a wizard Harry. No need to ask for a review every time.' Rebekah stood up and looked towards Harfleur. 'What do you think that was?'

Asking a man any question straight after sex is like asking a dog to play the piano. I had no idea, and I didn't care. We headed back towards the hotel.

Everyone was standing outside Olive's cottage. They had also heard the noise. Vic was trying to explain how a cannon worked.

'It's a big, long grey pipe. You pack the powder into the bottom of the canon, then load it with an iron ball. When the powder is lit it causes a great fire and sends the ball out of the canon as fast as an arrow. The ball flies for at least three hundred yards and will hit knock anything out. It reminds me of the passage from Luke, "And I saw Satan fall like lightning from Heaven" I am afraid the future of warfare will be a thing of terrible beauty.'

I believed him. It was a lethal weapon that could be fired by an idiot. A sword and an arrow had to be practised for years to be able to use it properly.

Olive turned Rebekah.

'Lucky you weren't sucking him off again when the big bang happened. You would have a face like a plasterers boots.' Rebekah had no idea what she was talking about. Arthur explained that Rebekah was his niece from England. Olive raised her hands to apologise.

'So sorry my little pickle of delight. I thought you was the hooker that gave Harry a nighttime nosh on the ship.'

At that moment I knew paradise was lost. I was just about to explain how the lack of food, the manuscript with the monkey skull, the wine and the drugs and the motion of the boat and being mistaken for a doctor…all perfectly reasonable excuses, when Rebekah punched me in the face. The bloody canon also fired again at the same time. Rebekah walked off.

Pieshop told Arthur to make sure she got back safely. There was nothing I could say or do until she had calmed down. If she did not take me back, I had no one to blame but myself. Vic said that a woman's love is like an hourglass with a crack in it. If you don't do anything to protect it, eventually all the sand will be gone, along with the woman. Tony was more succinct.

'You've really fucked up there.'

Chapter 21

I'm only sad in a natural way
   The Style Council, Paris Match (piano version)

I went back to the shed and let my thoughts run away with me while I lay motionless on the floor. Arthur finally came back.

'Give it a few days, son. I told her what had happened, but I think you need to realise women are not the same as men.'

'I know that.'

Really,' Arthur replied. 'You know that they want different things in a relationship, such as protection and laughter and honesty, not just sex.'

I sat back up. 'Hang on, Artie. All you've done is bang birds since you've joined. How come it works for you?'

'I may be a liar and a thief,' he replied, 'But I'm an honest one. I always tell women what's on my mind.'

Maybe that was it. Just tell her how I am feeling whether its good or bad. Would that make me more like Arthur? I spent the rest of the night worrying about my future.

The next few days were agony. Rebekah avoided me. I practiced my archery, hitting the bullseye several times, but I did not care. I studied medicine, ready to cut limbs off without flinching. I dug pits by myself, just to use up all my energy so I could sleep. I let Arthur cut my hair short, the same as nearly every man on the camp. Pieshop kept telling me I was an idiot for letting her go. Not only was she very attractive, but she also had a good heart. I had to watch as she smiled and laughed with other young men.

When Dr Culpepper had seen another physician set up a small leech farm, he wanted the hide of a creature to breed maggots. Arthur said there were some wild boar tracks in a nearby forest a couple of miles away. I said I would go. The others decided to come with me. Boars could only by killed by royal command. Technically that made us outlaws. But as we were not French, we didn't give a shiny shit.

We worked as a team, tracking the boars to their feeding grounds. The plan was for me or Pieshop to kill one. At this point I have another confession. I had only ever killed rabbits, squirrels, rats, and a fish once, but that was more by luck than anything else. A boar was slightly different. They were big ugly bastards.

As the group moved towards the centre of a clearing, I waited on a track until I saw an adult male. It was huge, as big as a lion, with small tusks like an elephant, and as angry as a cornered cat with ringworms. It had smelled us in the air (most likely Arthur, who had been pissing vinegar since we got here).

I had lost sight of the others. I knew they were close as I could hear them beating away in the bushes (probably Icky, the rascal). Slowly, I raised my longbow, hoping to get a clear shot. I pulled my arrow back just enough to feel the tension in my arm. I glanced to the left as a pheasant flew up towards a branch. When I turned back, the wild boar was charging directly towards me.

The creature moved fast. The only thing standing in its way was me. I pointed at the area just behind its skull. My courage failed and I fired while it was still some distance away. The arrow hit the creature near its hind legs. The boar kept coming. There was a snarl. I jumped into a bed of thorns. The boar ran past. Then it squealed and seemed to jump and stumble before it stopped just a few feet away. It was not my arrow that had killed the beast. A stake was impaled in the front of its chest.

Pieshop appeared further down the track. He quickly pierced the boar's heart with a knife, then admonished me for letting the animal suffer, and wasting an arrow. I looked at the boar. Pieshop had made a trap by placing a sharpened stake into the ground and tying it to some twine. As the boar ran past me, Pieshop had pulled the twine, and the wooden stake had pierced into the creature's body. I looked at its hind leg. My arrow had caused damage, but we might have spent hours trying to track it down before it would have collapsed. It was certainly a big thing. Better this old creature be killed than its son.

There is something else about wild boars. They absolutely stink. I mean, they really stink. The phrase "Happy as a pig in shit" comes to mind. We cut branches and took the boar back on a stretcher to Olive's hut rather than the camp. We hung it over a beam. Ideally, we should have left if for a few days and then skinned it, but Culpepper wanted the hide, plus a layer of fat on it. The magots were going to be used to clean soldiers wounds and stop them going sceptic. Tony sharpened his knife and took care of the boar. We got some thick cuts and added spices and pickled onions to make a stew. We all agreed that the boar should be shared out and given away to the locals. Derryck spent the rest of the night working out how much money we could make if we killed a boar every week and sold it in the camp.

 The hide was rolled and taken back to Culpepper. I saw Rebekah. I was not going to take no for an answer. She was going to hear me beg for forgiveness whether she liked it or not. She stood in silence as I explained what had happened. I handed her a muslin cloth filled with meat.

'For you,' I said. 'To remind you of the good times.'

'Is it a boars willy?' She asked.

I decided to leave. As I reached the tent door, she called out to me.

'Harry.' She threw a piece of thick wet meat. It landed right in the middle of my face with a splat. As it dribbled down and dropped onto the floor I was left with a stain on my cheeks. More silence. She finally laughed.

I told her that I had been an idiot. She asked me why I had done it. I blamed the wine. She then had a go at me for cutting my hair short, as she preferred it long. I asked if we could start courting again. She said she didn't know at the moment and would think about it.

I went outside and stretched the hide across the wooden beams. The flies were buzzing around my face. It was the golden fleece in reverse. With every step of my journey, I seemed to be going backwards. As I nailed the creature to the cross, I found the mark where I had hit the creature and caused it to suffer. I needed to improve my aim. I needed Rebekah.

Chapter 22

I was mightily troubled with a looseness, and feeling for a chamber-pot, there was none; so, I was forced in this strange house to rise and shit in the chimney twice.
  Samuel Pepys, The Diary of Samuel Pepys

Over the next few weeks, we got quite a few kills in, until the locals started complaining that the sheep and goats were going missing. The Duke of York made poaching punishable with two days in the stocks. But the knights continued to go out hunting because they classed it as a sport. We went out and set up rabbit traps while digging cesspits. Pieshop would often go to the local church and pray, giving his rabbit to the local priest. Pieshop would speak about having to carry his suffering. He said every man must wait in penitence for his sins to come home to roost. The priest would tell him that without struggle we would never find our true strength. Pieshop's son would sometimes come over to us if he could get away from Sir Tate. As he was just a boy, Olive would cook him snails in garlic. I tried one, and it didn't taste too bad.

 I still went around acting as the lad who liked a laugh, always smiling, likes going out and a kicking the balls. But inside I was broken. The only way I could define it was that I was not happy, and not sad. I thought about Rebekah more since she had left me than when we were together. I couldn't avoid seeing her, but she simply saw me as a friend. I kept working, playing, and hunting, but I still couldn't sleep. I would ask Vic to play sad songs, even when everyone else groaned that they had heard it already. Whenever I closed my eyes, she would appear as a vision. I even dreamt about things that had never happened. I was a knight in shining armour, and she was the damsel in distress. It always ended up with me winning her heart. I would wake up wishing for sleep to come back as soon as possible.

The feast day of Saint Augustine came and went. The army had been having a pretty easy time so far. The French soldiers in the fort had enough to eat and drink, even though no one could understand how. The English soldiers in the field were not getting killed. The locals were happy to sell or barter whatever they had with us. The sun it shoneth every day. My arms and face turned brown as I felt my muscles growing.

A few men had been injured using the siege machines. Splinters mostly. I was beginning to think some of them were coming over to the physician's tent just to speak to Rebekah. The biggest danger in Harfleur so far was getting lice or the clap. Dirty Dave, the Welsh sheep shagger, was rumoured to have caught both at the same time.

When Rebekah did finally speak to me, it was about her uncle Arthur's cough. I spoke about his helmet and how he rarely took it off. One of the knights servants walked past and said hello to Rebekah, who smiled and said hello back. My stomach twisted in knots, and my mouth dried. I would not ask who he was. No need to be jealous. I am not going to ask. There is no need whatsoever for me to ask.

'Who was that?'

'Just a friend.'

My next thought was to go up and punch him. 'I miss you.' I don't know if I wanted her to reply or not. She gave me the look. Not the look that says you are a likeable idiot. It was the look that said you are just an idiot. She was called away to help another nurse make bandages. I went to help Dr Culpepper, as he had a new theory about the healing powers of garlic. All I could think about was the other young lad. He didn't look strong enough to fire a longbow. Perhaps he didn't need to. War finally came to me on 8th September 1415, the feast day of Saint Mary.

We were ordered to the general's tent. Pieshop told us to bring our shovels. He had seen more cannons arrived, and chances are they wanted people to man them. Arthur coughed loudly as we waited outside. The man in the tent was a gruff looking old soldier called General Bates. He looked at us and smiled.

'Thought you would bring your shovels just in case I put you on cannon duties?' He stopped at Pieshop. 'You look like an old soldier, I bet that it was your idea. Well, I am offering extra pay for it.' He noticed Derryck show an interest, and then he noticed the helmet on Arthur's head. 'Who are you meant to be; Thor's toilet brush?' He continued smiling. 'You have all been in the latrine unit for a few months, digging holes?'
We all nodded. He stopped smiling. 'Unfortunately, for you men I have nothing to offer but bad news. An archer has died of dysentery. I don't want to start a panic among the ranks. I am asking you to volunteer to bury the man because no one will be surprised to see you with the shovels. If there is an outbreak, I will have to set up burial teams. Do any of you have any religious training?'

'I do,' said Pieshop.
General Bates nodded. He asked Pieshop to stay and for the rest of us to come back at sunset. We walked out of the tent.

'Great,' said Icky. 'I've come all this way to sleep with lots of women, and I end up working for a Master Bates.'
Vic nodded. 'They say he keeps a tough grip on his unit.'
   We saw a cannon and went over to look.
'This must be it lads,' said Vic. 'The future of warfare. A giant bilge pipe.'

It was certainly a strange beast. Encased in a cart with solid wooden wheels, was a long and extremely thick cast iron tube with a bulbous tip; dirty grey in colour and must have weighed at least nine horses.

'Just like an elephant's penis,' said Arthur.'
The Welsh soldier Paz came over and patted the cannon. 'Want to see this little baby in action?'

Three men were needed to take it into position just a few hundred yards from the wall of the fort. The process of loading the cannon with wadding and gunpowder, pushing it down, then loading the cannonball, took quite a while. The French soldiers on the turrets taunted us by shouting insults. Vic tried to translate.

'I think they are saying that we smell of elderberries, which to be fair, after drinking elderberry tea, we probably do. And that they fart in our general direction.' He turned to us. 'We need to put Arthur downwind and let him rip one of those elephant sized pickled onion farts. That will wipe the smiles from their faces.'

We stood back as one man was chosen to light the cannon. We stood even further back when those who had helped pack the cannon went and stood behind us. The lone man walked up holding a long smoking faggot stick. He placed the tip on the rear of the cannon. There was a spark. I was sure I felt the cannon move before I heard the bang. The ball flew out into space, and hit the stone wall. As the smoke cleared, we could see it had taken a few chinks out of the thick wall. The French soldiers clapped.

We decided to walk around the fort as Derryck wanted to see if there was money to be made. As we began to walk along the river Sienne the ground turned into marshland. There was no need for the English to guard this area. Arthur went for a whizz and said he had found something. A small man-made stream which had been dammed at the river by wooden slats which could be removed. The water would then run into a culvert in the fort wall. Pieshop noticed that this stream had no reeds whatsoever. Someone was dredging it on a regular basis. It would certainly be easy to wait for high tide, then send food down the stream and into the fort. We headed back towards the camp.

When we went back to the other side, I noticed that although the surrounding fields had become parched over the summer, grass and nettles were growing in abundance near the wall. A small grill allowed a wet brown sludge to ooze out from the fort and dry in the sun. The French were using the tide to bring in food on one side, and pumping out their sewage on the side where the English were camped. Come the first heavy rain, men could find themselves in deep trouble.

We spoke to General Bates. He couldn't change plans, as more cannons had arrived, but he would tell King Henry. Plus, the dry weather was still holding out. He told us that three more men had shown the symptoms of dysentery. On the advice of the royal doctor, the duke of York was going to put each man in a different physician's tent. That would mean Rebekah would be helping someone who had been infected.

Dr Culpepper's tent could fit ten beds. Rebekah was making a herbal drink for the only patient.

'Culpepper's not happy,' she said. 'He wanted everyone infected to be kept together in one tent isolated from the camp.'

'Are you safe?'

She nodded. 'I drink apple cider vinegar every day to keep the flux away. Do you?' As I nodded, she continued. 'It tastes like horse piss, doesn't it?

'You made it for me,' I replied.

'I pick the leaves from that field full of horses.' She finally smiled.

We were interrupted by the sound of cannon fire. Rebekah rubbed her hands with a white rag.

'I hope we can go home soon.'

'One man has already died. They want us to bury him.' This was hardly my idea of wooing her.

She thought for a moment. 'Make sure he's wrapped up well. Wear a mask that has been soaked in urine and covered with wood ash.' She handed me a cup. 'Take this.'

I took a gulp. 'That tastes like piss as well. What is it?'

She looked into the cup. 'That genuinely is piss.' She got some rags and poured the urine over them, then went to the fireplace and covered the rags with ash. She told me to hang them on a line to dry (like the love letters I should have sent her, I thought). We said our goodbyes. I wanted to kiss her, but I was too afraid to lose her again. I went back to join the others.

We moved out just before dark. Dressed in our hooded cloaks, with ash-coloured masks covering our mouths, we had become death, the destroyer of worlds. The body was wrapped in a horse blanket. We put it onto a handcart. The young knight's servant came over and told us he wanted the blanket back. Tony told him to fuck off. If he wanted it, he could come with us and take from the body after we had placed it in the ground. A few months ago, Tony would have quietly done as he was ordered.

We travelled along a path, following the North Star until we saw a small church. In the moonlight shadow of a yew tree, we dug a shallow grave and rolled the body into the earth. Then we went back to Olive's. We gave her the blanket and told her to soak it in hot vinegar water. She gave us some wine and made a prayer for the unknown soldier. Our first death. Later, so many men would become ill that the army ran out of blankets, and so many men died they were buried without any prayers given.

Chapter 23

The terror of being judged sharpens the memory.
 George Eliot, Middlemarch

Something happened which seems to be of such celestial synchronicity that I wonder even today if more than just mere chance was guiding my life. I met my old mate Rodney. Having now been a soldier for several months, he had filled out a bit. He was proud of his armour, although not happy that he had to have a haircut. He had joined the newly formed artillery unit. His nickname in the regiment was "Fringe". The pay was better, and you were given your own tent to keep the gunpowder dry. It was almost as good as being a knight. He tapped my longbow and said the age of chivalry was over.

'Then allow me to retort,' I said. 'I've shagged a bird.' Rodney laughed. 'Me too, some drunken bint in a sailor's rest home. Greek style, bit of butter, straight in. Bosh. And now I'm here I've heard there is a proper tasty little sort working as a nurse. Becky, her name is. I'm going to have a wander around later, see if I can give her some of the Rodney charm.'
The idea of her being with someone who knew me was worse than if she went out with a stranger.

'She doesn't like men with short hair.'
Rodney looked at me. 'Well, it looks like you and me will both be doing a stander-upper in our bushes tonight.'

We met again the next day. Rodney stood around one cannon as it was filled with wadding, then gunpowder, then salt peter, then the cannon ball. Again, we all stood back as the man chosen to hold the lighted fag walked over to the cannon. There was a moment of pregnant anticipation. As he placed the smoking tip it on the bulbous barrel, I looked over at the fort wall. Someone said the usual joke about Jericho.

A wave of shock knocked me backwards. I heard the bang. But it was not the same as last time. The noise had been so loud it almost split my ears. Smoke went in all directions. As it cleared from my eyes, I could see the cannon itself had exploded. The back end had been rendered open. The two legs of the man nearest the cannon were on the floor, but the rest of his body had gone. Another soldier was covered in blood. Derryck was on the ground. Someone else started screaming in pain. Someone else was clutching their forearm. Arthur climbed out from under a cart, put his Viking helmet back on and brushed himself down.

I turned to Rodney to tell him if he thought I was joining the artillery unit he was having a laugh. He seemed to be standing there with that same gormless look on his face that all sixteen-year-old boys do when asked about their prospects with work or women. His eyes were open, but they might just as well have been closed. He stayed staring at nothing. I called his name and asked him if he was Ok. He began to fall backwards. I caught him but could not hold him. I called his name. He fell to the ground. His head turned. Now he was staring at blades of grass. I called his name. Derryck came over. I called his name. Derryck moved me away and checked my friend. I called his name. Derryck found the wound. A thin piece of shrapnel smaller than an arrowhead had gone straight into his heart, killing him instantly. I turned his face and called his name. His hair cut short, he silently stared at the sun.

Gently, we carried his body to Dr Culpepper. Derryck went and got Rodney's belongings before they were stolen. I did not want anything. Derryck said he would sell the armour and give the money to Rodney's mum when we returned. I wanted to bury my friend in front of the Knight's encampment. That way they would know how the young men of England were willing to die in some foreign land for the sake of King and country.

Instead, we carried him to a church and asked for a Christian burial. The priest was not so sure as he had heard soldiers were dying of dysentery. If we wanted a full service and burial, it would be expensive. Even though some of them had never known him, all of my friends chipped in to pay for the funeral because they knew it was important to me. I have never forgotten that moment of kindness and respect. I promised myself I would help them no matter what.

Rebekah knew about me and Rodney. I had told her all the funny stories about me and him arsing about as kids, standing on the Thames when it was frozen, trying to impress girls, walking the streets in the dark, our first time getting drunk together, and how close we were. She found me walking among the tents trying to buy as many bottles of wine as I could. She did not scold me. Instead, she took me to sit under a tree on a hill. I drank the bottle as I told her I had been an idiot and even if our relationship was over, I just didn't want to be alone tonight. She held onto me until I fell asleep.

Chapter 24

Baldrick: "Have you got a cunning plan, Sir?"
Blackadder: "Yes I have, and it's so cunning you could brush your teeth with it!"
   Blackadder.

After being in France for over a month it was clear that if there was a plan, the plan was not going to plan. The number of those coming down with dysentery was going up all the time. Death soon became part of daily life. In the end we started to dig mass graves. Those who could afford it were shipped back to England. On the feast day of Moses, so many men died some of them were slipped into the river, only to be washed up on the beach by the next high tide. We began losing nearly a hundred men a day to disease. The only positive was that those who lived obtained better longbows, better swords, clothes, and armour. We wondered when the French were going to attack.

It was said that King Charles sat in Paris covered in feathers because he believed he was made of glass. The generals at the palace were ordered to check horoscopes, find magical artifacts, and help build a model city that was going to be the heart of a new European empire rather than draw up battle plans. The politicians that surrounded him were happy to keep the siege going. Talk of invaders created fear, and a society that lived in fear were more complaint to new rules, and more taxes. None of this helped us. If we destroyed the fort and the French then surrendered, we had won a pile of broken bricks. It would be the same as knocking down an ancient statue in St. Albans and declaring we had beaten the Romans. We took a break from digging out a long burial pit. Vic pointed the ivory tusk on my longbow.

'Remember your story of Hannibal? He travelled all the way across the Alps with elephants to fight the Romans, only to lose because the Roman general, Fabius Maximus, turned it into a war of attrition. He avoided fighting a major battle, and instead waited until Hannibal's army became weaker by the day and picked off small groups of them until the army was easily defeated.'

'There is a difference,' said Pieshop. 'Maximus was a great general who used tactics to defeat the enemy; whereas King Charles has as much military acumen as a cold sausage called Bernard.' He pointed towards the fort. 'But somehow, they have not run out of food and water. If we could cut off the supply, we can speed up their defeat.'

Icky leaned on his shovel. 'Why us. Theres a couple of thousand men here who can go look.'

'The locals know who we are,' Pieshop replied. 'They will think we are on the thieve, on the pull, or on a graveyard shift. I reckon they are smuggling goods into that fort using prostitutes.'

'Give me five minutes,' said Icky.

Later that night we went through the camp to speak to an engineer who claimed he could get us into the fort. Nigel Fairservice invited us into his tent. On a table were a series of drawings. His idea was simple. He would stitch together hundreds of feathers onto two large wooden wings. This frame would then be strapped to me, where I would then be fired from a catapult, and the wings would allow me to fly over the fort. It had all been worked out with mathematical precision, including the type of wood and feathers that would give me maximum height and distance. The best thing would be to launch from a south easterly position and land in the English camp. I then realised something.

'Wait…go back a bit. *Me?*'

'I would do it myself,' the Nigel replied. 'But unfortunately, I've got a touch of Ceasars revenge. Very loose and runny. Quite unsuitable for the element of surprise. My feather machine almost worked with Wee Willy McClusky, the dancing dwarf from Congleton. Lovley man. Never wore anything under his kilt. Stayed away from stinging nettles. I like to think that he is still somewhere up there now.' Nigel looked at the roof of the tent. 'Fly free, little Willy, fly free.' He wiped a tear from his cheek and gave me a gentle punch. So, you young aeronaut, are you ready for some fun and hi-jinks?'

'No,' I replied. 'This is batshit crazy. For a start, if it worked, you should be able to take off from the ground. Next, you would have to take off in daylight, and all you would see are the tops of roofs, not what was inside. Then you would get spotted, the crossbow men on the turrets would have an easy shot, especially if their covered their bolts in burning tar.' I looked at the pile of wood and feathers. 'How did the war get to this? A tent full of crack pots trying to promote me from emptying the piss pots by turning me into a French hot pot. You would be better off taking one of the ships sails, tying a man to it, and letting that rise above the fort.' I left. For the first time in my life, I had more faith in my own intuition than some adult who claimed to know more than me. I thought of a different plan and told the others.

Before dawn broke, we crawled up to the side of the wall which had the river Sienne running past. Tony had a dancing fit behind a bush. A guard on patrol at the top of the tower called down to us.

'Hey, Englishman. I see you playing with yourself in the bushes. Go home Icky Custard and give your hand a rest. You only get a bucket and a half. Even in litres that is still not much.'

Tony and Arthur stepped out. 'We've come to join your army.' The guard looked down at Arthurs helmet. 'Do you mean the Roman army?'

Arthur called up to him. 'I'm what they call a swarthy Viking.'

'Swampy?'

'Swarthy,' said Arthur. 'Rugged, like a Greek statue hewn from solid marble.' He ignored Tony shaking next to him. More guards looked down as the first man laughed. 'And I think you have lost your marbles. You look about as tough as a Greek salad. Go away and take your dancing monkey with you.'

'Minkey?' Arthur called back.

'Monkey,' said the guard. 'Surely you have monkeys in England. I have seen the eyebrows of your ladies.'

'I am sleeping with a French woman.'

The man called out to another guard. 'Hey Francois, you didn't tell me your mother is back.' He then called down to Arthur. 'Who is it?'

Arthur called up. 'She's a big woman with bad breath and spotty arse.'

The guards in the tower conversed with each other. The man then spoke. 'Monsieur, this is France, you will have to narrow it down a bit more.'

As the guard and Arthur argued over the qualities of their native women, Pieshop and I had moved down to the small stream. There was movement in the bushes. We got closer. People on a boat were placing baskets of food and wine into the river and pushing them towards the hole in the wall. A lamp flashing three times on the boat was enough for the culvert to be raised.

In the morning, we went down to where the river meets the sea. The sewage from the locals also came this way. The smell was horrendous. I waded through with a net to get as many shellfish and oysters as I could. We cleaned them up and put them in a basket. That night we got Olive to take the basket up to the river. We flashed a lamp three times. The culvert was raised, and the basket disappeared. Those in the fort were going to get a taste of their own medicine, although it could not be as bad as our camp. We did the same for the next few nights.

By the middle of September, the English army was suffering from such a plague that there was simply no time for everyone to receive treatment. Having been surrounded by shit before France, we had become accustomed to it by the time we arrived here. As we were also a burial party, we were allowed to go out to look for grave sites, and hunt food. Tony had fallen in love with garlic and put it into everything. At first it a bit too much, but now I really liked it. Rebekah kept us supplied with apple cider vinegar. It helped save our lives. Only Arthur seemed to look a bit peaky. His cough was getting worse, and he was having to travel further out to nick anything decent. Our greatest concern was being trapped in France over the Winter. The sun was setting earlier and earlier every day. Soon no ship would cross the channel until the Spring due to the storms.

The natives were also becoming restless. Having first watched us with a mixture of boredom and fascination, now there was an element of contempt. They had been happy to sell us food and wine on the basis we would soon pack up and leave. But the idea of us being here for Christmas, thousands of men invading a foreign land, away from their own rules and culture, they knew it would only lead to trouble.

There was also something else. The physicians were getting a strange new phenomenon to deal with. Men were being ambushed close to the camp. Rather than be killed, they had the first two fingers from their right hand cut off. Not only did it mean they could never use their longbow again, but it also meant more resources being used on someone who was no longer an effective soldier.

If the wound was fresh and clean, the patient would be given alcohol and hemp. The hand would then be strapped so that it could not move, and I would hold them down as Dr Culpepper pressed a red-hot poker against each stubbed finger. The men would scream and curse or black out. It was the only way we knew to stop gangrene. Those who recovered were offered a voyage home. King Henry gave the order that no one was to walk around the town alone. This was difficult as many men had formed relationships with the locals, either through extra work or trading goods, while many others had fallen in love.

Spending so much time in the physician's tent also meant working with Rebekah. I realised just how good she was at her job. She knew more than me about plants and just seemed to pick everything up so quickly. I started to teach her how to read and wrote. I decided to be honest with her about everything. I told her how I was feeling, about all my fears and dreams. Other young men would go out of their way to speak to her. I can't blame them for that. As well as being very attractive when she wore that white wenches outfit, she had a kind of glow that only those with a good soul have. I still felt a bit jealous. But to lose her again would break my heart. I would continue to bear my suffering while we were all waiting for something else to break.

Chapter 25

May all your doughnuts look like Fanny's.
  Johnnie Craddock (husband of Fanny Craddock, TV chef)

There was something in the air. A sense of an ending. No one could really describe it, but we all felt that the days were not the same as how we lived just a short time ago. King Henry was now leading the operations. The diggers had reached under the fort wall. The culvert on the far side was blocked, meaning no more food into the fort. All the cannons fired at the wall above the main gates. The siege machines were adapted to catapult bales of rotten fish into the fortified town. Vic looked up at the sky above the walls.

'The air hangs heavy like a sullen wine.'

'It's probably all those pickled onions Arthur's been eating,' said Derryck.

A messenger came out of the gates. The town councillors asked for a parley with Henry. It was agreed that if the French army had not arrived by the 23$^{rd\ of}$ September, the councillors would surrender the town. This was the day of Saint Maurice, the Roman general who refused to execute captured Christians. Henry agreed. He then decided to carry out a full attack on the 22nd. Henry wanted a victory even if there was no official battle.

The day we stormed the barricades was also the day of the first real storm since we had been here. Summer was over. Although hard to light because of the rain, the cannons breached the wall above the gates. The tunnel underneath caused a large part of wall to collapse. The Knights rode into the fort and through the streets shouting for victory. The foot soldiers were ordered to take prisoners. The archers went from room to room looking for anything valuable. The news was sent back that the English army had just won the war, and had gained nothing.

I watched the soldiers celebrating, more in relief than triumph. Pieshop put his arm around his son's shoulder and smiled as the rain fell on his face. I went looking for Rebekah.

Tending to the Knights was the best nursing job because it meant you were well fed and could get shipped home. But Rebekah always wanted to help those from the lowest ranks. They were just as good as Kings, she would say. The medicine that she made herself to give to those in need meant that some spoke of her being a witch. As such, she could walk through the camp at night without fear. Becky must have been propositioned by every soldier on their first day in the infirmary, and her bum squeezed more times than a spotty teenagers face. There is something about nurses uniforms I suppose (it certainly works for me), and men just wanting to believe they were still men. But after a while the men, some who had wives and daughters back home, were very protective of her. One old archer had the rule that you didn't swear in front of women, and woe betide anyone who did in front of his Becky.

I found her trying to set up a tent, while men, too weak to help, looked on. She told me off for walking around in the rain without my hood up, then proceeded to get soaked herself as we helped move the soldiers under canvas. I noticed the bones in her fingers were more prominent. The rabbits and deer I had been catching for her; she had been giving to her patients.

'Have you eaten today?'
She shook her head. 'Have you?'

Once all the men were inside, Rebecca hung a lamp under the awning and gave me a piece of seeded bread. We stood listening to the rain. She told me that Sir Tate had set me up by getting one of the hookers to seduce me, but she never went any further because she felt guilty. I told her that I wouldn't have done anything else.

   Down in the fields fires were burning where the wall had been breached. I put my cloak around her. As I did so I slowly and gently kissed her on the forehead. She remarked I had finally started to grow a beard, although she was still not happy that I had cut my hair so short. I blamed her uncle Arthur. She ran her fingers over my head and smiled.

   'It's a good job you've got me in your life.'
I stopped her. 'Bex, you're not just in my life, you are my life. It goes me, you, and then everyone else. You are the kindest soul I have ever met. I love that you work hard and care so much. And you are the most beautiful woman I have ever seen. There is not a day that goes by when I don't think about you. The only reason I sleep at night is so I can dream about you. And if I never say thank you enough for being here it's because I'm a man and I'm an idiot. And I wish I had a better job and more money and all that other stuff just so I could give you everything you want. But everything I have is yours, including my heart. I'm not good with words, so all I can say is that I want to hold you in my arms, but I'm scared because I don't know if I could ever let you go.'

   We kissed. We kissed as the fires in the camp burned into the night. She held my hand as we ran down towards the shore. As we got close to the hut, I picked her up and carried her. I had grown stronger; she had grown lighter.

   I had made friends who were willing to fight for me, and I knew I would risk my own life to save theirs. And best of all, I had met Becky. Now that the war was over, we could start thinking about the future. I walked through the rain and did not want to put her down.

The shed was empty. I slowly took her clothes off, kissing each part of her body. I took my clothes off and stood behind her as my hands and lips searched her wet skin. This was me naked and happy. I smiled and told her I loved her. I took hold her wrists and led her to a bed of straw. She climbed on top of me, feeling my chest and shoulders as I thrusted my tongue into her mouth and she grinded onto my hips. I climbed on top of her, placed my forearms tight against her waist her and kissed her nipples. I told her how much she made me hard. Somewhere in the distance the soldiers were celebrating.

After, we looked for something to eat. I found Icky's book and we looked at the pictures. There was one image we both stared at. In the shadow of the lamplight, Rebekah climbed onto a bale of straw and got on her knees, raising her firm arse in the air. It was at this point that I invented a new word, "Wow." I had never said it before and had no idea where it came from, but it fitted. Those two, firm, ripe figgy puddings, and a slice of sponge cake wedged in-between her thighs, was God's way of saying, "Here you go lads, this is what Christmas Day and your birthday at the same time looks like". I felt like Jesus. I know I slowly called out his name. I don't know why her in this position tightened my bolt so strenuously, and I didn't care. I was sixteen years old, and this was the greatest moment of my life. There was something very primal between us that night. As the rain fell hard on the roof, a thin layer of sweat rose from our bodies. I held her waist and pulled her hair. My heart pounded over and over again until it felt as though the universe had been created in my body.

Afterwards we spooned with her resting her head on my arm until she fell asleep. Every smooth curve of her hips and chest seemed to gently rise and fall like warm waves on a soft beach. How strange that even the dips and folds of her ear, cheek, neck, and shoulders, were more beautiful to me than every star in the sky.

Many years ago, a woman in Valance Road gave birth to twins. I remember my mum taking me to see them. I sort of understood that they had been in the woman's stomach all this time, and I wondered what it must be like to be that close to each other. Now I knew. As shards of daylight broke through the holes in the ceiling, I knew my boyhood was over.

Derryck came into the shed with Olive. She had been expecting Arthur back, but he never returned. We got dressed and walked up to the fort. It was surprising that Arthur was not among the soldiers, as he really loved to steal. He said it was what he had been born for. We found the others. They could not remember when they last saw him. Tony thought he might be in the knights camp cutting their hair and shaving them to look good for the official surrender. We checked, but Pieshop's son had not seen him. He was not in any of the physicians' tents. Dr Culpepper said that he had given him some honey for his cough, but that was two days ago. We kept expecting to find him trying to steal the used cannonballs and sell them back to the English. But Arthur was nowhere to be seen. We checked the graves. He was not among the dead. We agreed to go out and search for him.

Our first problem was General Bates. Since the fort had surrendered there had been a lot of complaints about looting and drunken debauchery. The knights who wanted us to lay our lives on the line for their glory had set up a line of security because they wanted to take everything back home for themselves. Vic pointed out that we had been one of the few units that had worked non-stop since we had arrived (late), and that we were all willing to be on the last ship home if he let us go find our friend. Derryck handed over a French gold candle snuff. General Bates asked us what we needed. Pieshop told him three days, and if we had not returned by then we could all be hanged for desertion. Bates warned us to be careful, and that we could not take our shovels, just in case we were going to bury any stolen property. He also told us the French King had still not signed the terms of surrender. Technically we were still at war.

 We left the camp that day. Pieshop's son was granted permission to join us, to bring back any horses. It had not been a great campaign. There had been no major battle that we would one day sit around and tell our children about. There had been no enemy to face. Our trials had been small in the big scheme of things, a mere footnote in history. But we had formed a bond during training, we learned we could push our bodies further than we had done before, and we had survived. All we had to do was find our friend and then we could all go home.

Chapter 26

It is only when you meet someone of a different culture from yourself that you begin to realise what your own beliefs really are.
    George Orwell, The Road to Wigan Pier.

We headed up along the river Seine. It was still raining. The boat yards and sailors' huts were silent. There were six hills about three miles away. We knew that Arthur had been scouting the area to see what was worth pinching.

'Do you think he's done a runner?' Icky asked.
Derryck shook his head. 'Blimey. The poor old sod couldn't run a tin bath.'
Icky continued his train of thought. 'But what if last night while everyone was fighting, he's nicked a load of jewellery and had it on his toes. He's got a day's start. And right now, the king is opening the royal box to put on his crown and sees a tin helmet with a pair of horns on it.'

'He wouldn't,' said Derryck.

'But why?'
Derryck stopped. 'Because Artie's our pal. Do you know what he said to me a few nights ago; that this is the bestest time he's ever had with his clothes on.'

'That's not much,' said Vic. 'Have you seen Olive?'
 Derryck disagreed. 'The thing about us is, we're all a little bit wavy, but we're all straight, no offence Tony. We look after each other. That's why I know he hasn't done a runner. Because if he had half inched the crown jewels, he would have told us about it.'

I had to agree. I was the youngest of the original group. Arthur was the oldest. We were sometimes seen as the outsiders. Pieshop taught me how to fight, Derryck taught me how to be confident, Vic how to be an artist, Icky about women (kind of), and Tony how to cook. To me, Arthur was a magician. He could disappear and then suddenly turn up with something in his hand. As Derryck once said, Arthur may have looked like he came from the bottom of the slag heap to those who did not know him; but to us he was a diamond geezer. The rain finally stopped.

We passed a farm where he had taken a chicken, a vineyard where we knew he had stolen wine, and a gate house that didn't have any led on the roof. There was a chateau nearby. Further along the hill there was an orchard of walnuts. He had brought back a bag of those one day, but there was no sign of him. We had reached about four miles from Harfleur and still not found him. We decided to keep walking up towards the ridge of a hill.

'What are you going to do when you get back home?' Tony asked Derryck.

'Get some of that Ophelia bird,' Derryck replied. ''ll start by taking her out for a nice meal, somewhere fancy, with spoons, you know, proper high class. I'll order a bottle of wine, the really good stuff, at least six weeks old. Then I will tell her how beautiful she looks, even though she's been around the cathedral more times than the Bishops dog, and how that missing tooth gives her a certain charm when she smiles. Then I will find a local inn that's got a bed, gently take her upstairs, lay her down, kiss her body, tell her how even the flabby bits are sexy, and how naughty I want to be, wait till I've been given the nod, and then absolutely smash her.'

Icky was impressed. 'You're quite the wordsmith when it comes to women.'

'And what about after that?' Tony asked.

Derryck thought about it. 'Well, I'm not as young as I used to be, so I might be an hour before I'm ready to go again, unless she's got a naughty nuns outfit or a or a sexy maiden uniform with her.'

'No. After all this. What are you going to do in the future?'

'Work hard, get rich, climb up the old social ladder, move out to the country, somewhere nice, like Neasden.' Derryck turned to Tony. 'What about you?'

Tony was probably the quietest of the group. With his uncontrollable shake and nervous swearing, his choices were limited. After we had walked a few paces in silence, the conversation started again.

'I've got it. Why don't you join me,' said Derryck. 'I was telling my mate Lofty Cohen and his brother Jack about how I could get a couple of stalls selling different stuff all in the same market and set my own prices. I need someone like you to run the butcher's section.'

'Join me,' said Icky. 'I might open up a little business empire selling hemp cakes. I can do the chemistry, but I need someone who knows how to cook. We could call it "Breaking Bread."'

Vic checked the horizon. 'Reginald Kincaid's travelling players have asked me to join them. But I would only go if they took you as well, Tony.'

'I know a few people in the city,' said Pieshop. 'Don't do anything until I see if I can get you a job in one of the big kitchens.'

Tony smiled as we headed through the trees. I don't think he knew what he wanted to do in the future. He was just happy he had friends around him right now.

At the top of the hill, we stopped. We all knew that Arthur would not have gone any further. In front of us was a valley and then a line of trees that went up another hill. Beyond that was a forest. None of us said anything for a while, not wishing to speak the truth, not wanting to turn back.

'I think he might have gone over that next hill,' said Tony. 'He knew we could all be going home soon. So, I think he would have gone as far as he could to make sure he hadn't missed anything.'

It was a few more miles, down and then up. We did it in silence. At the top of the next hill, we knew we would turn back. We could have turned back right now, but Tony's future was just in the distance. He started moving again. We followed.

The meadows here were filled with flowers that I did not recognise. I stopped to pick some for Rebekah. Icky started picking mushrooms. By the time we had got to the hill he had a large pouch full. He said they should be OK as cattle were grazing nearby. I looked over and saw a young shepherd boy sitting on the grass watching us. He was playing small pan pipes. They were not loud enough to warn anyone, so I waved as we kept moving. Strangely, the boy raised his hand and moved it across the sky, almost as if he was blessing me rather than waving back. Halfway up the hill I turned, but the boy had gone.

We found ourselves in unfamiliar surroundings. It was a wood. There were oaks, beeches, and Fir trees, none of them suitable for harvesting. There were berries and healing plants, but they would not produce a harvestable crop. I had the impression that it was a bit like a very large, slightly overgrown garden. Vic looked around.

'This is where Arthur would have come. He would have sussed out what they were farming here.'

Derryck leaned over. 'Have the French have suddenly got a taste for stinging nettles and pigeon shit?'

Vic shook his head and smiled. 'Truffles. The most expensive mushrooms in the world.'

We spread out to look for Arthur. The woods had patches of green where trees had been felled and then left. I walked along one fallen oak that must have been a hundred yards long. At the end the branches jutted out as if slain by a warrior from times past.

It was Tony that called out first. Then he called out again. A bit louder. Then louder still, but now he was running. I tried looking through the trees as he called out again. I put an arrow in my hand and followed the sound. Something appeared ahead of me. I lifted my longbow and took aim.

It was a dark-skinned Moor. I had seen a picture in a book but had never seen a real black man in the whole of England. I read that they came from Africa, and they believed in different Gods. What he was doing in a country filled with Crusaders and Catholics I did not know.

'Prester John, Prester John,' he kept saying to me.
I didn't know if that was his name or that he thought it was mine, but I did know he had Arthur's Viking helmet in his hand. The Moor stopped. The others were getting closer. He looked at me, and then at the arrowhead. I was standing in his way. He took a step towards me. I pulled my arrow back.

A wild boar came crashing through the undergrowth. Keeping its head down and tusks up, it charged towards us. The Moor found himself trapped in the middle of wild nature and a dangerous civilisation. He jumped out of the way. I took a step to the side, aimed, and hit the boar in its right front haunches. The arrow pierced the creature's lung and heart. The shaft broke as its legs buckled. The animal fell over itself and died. I took out another arrow and aimed again. The others appeared from the trees. They surrounded the Moor.

'He was hiding in the bushes,' said Tony. 'I only realised he was there when he moved after I had a shake and started pissing on his back. He's got Arthur's helmet.'

The Moor said something in a mixture of French and Spanish. Vic spoke to him. The Moor got down on his knees and pleaded with him over and over again. They had a brief conversation in which I could make out some words, but not all of them. Vic said something about us being English.

'He says he's not a French soldier,' said Vic. 'He's come here because he heard there was going to be a battle and he was looking for work.'

'As what?' Derryck asked.

The Moor said something. Vic looked at us. 'A gravedigger.'

Pieshop stepped forward and took the helmet. 'Where did he get this from?'

'He said he found it,' said Vic. 'Near two buffalos.'

Derryck took out his knife. 'Bollocks.'

The Moor spoke again.

'He said they might be,' said Vic. 'As they both had great big horns.'

The Moor saw the ivory clasp and became wild with excitement.

'Looky, looky, I have Elephant stone.'

He took out a long egg-shaped grey stone which was the size of his palm. The stone had been carved out in the middle and around were four symbols. The Moor kept calling it his Elephant Stone. He took out a small box and placed a metal rod into the hollow, and then a tiny arrow onto the rod.'

'It's a navigation stone,' said Vic. 'The arrow always points north, even when the north star can't be seen in the heavens.'

'Elephant Stone,' said the Moor.

I took it off him. The stone was incredibly light, nothing I had seen on any church buildings. I walked around in a circle, and the arrow always pointed in one direction.

'That way he can find east,' said Vic.

'Tell him not to bother,' said Derryck. 'Dagenham is a shit hole.'

Pieshop was not impressed. 'Can it tell us where to find Arthur, otherwise it's a fucking waste of time.'

He ordered the Moor to take his clothes off. Men are more likely not to hide secrets when naked.

At first the Moor seemed unsure of what was being asked. A group of men, in the woods, one of them a black man holding a large helmet, what could possibly go wrong. Pieshop pointed his knife at the Moor. The Moor took off his clothes until he had just his trousers on. Pieshop gestured for everything to come off. The Moor looked at me and kept saying something about the Elephant Stone. Pieshop stepped forward. The Moor took out a small leather pouch. There were coins, along with gold and silver jewellery. There was also Arthur's shaving blade and wet stone. The Moor said he had found them as well. Even Vic stopped smiling.

Derryck and Tony wanted to kill him on the spot. Pieshop said that we should make him take us to find the body first. Vic kept trying to calm the Moor down. The Moor kept asking for the Elephant stone back so he could pray. I noticed that the dead boar was staring at me. Flies were landing on its eyes and mouth. I felt sick. Pieshop put the jewellery back into the pouch, and the coins into his pocket. Then he ordered the Moor to pull his trousers down. Icky looked at the naked Moor and whispered under his breath. 'It's the size of an elephant's penis.'

Pieshop told the Moor he could either point out where Arthur was with his finger or his cock. The Moor kept talking about him being guarded by two creatures. Did he know the way? Yes, yes. The Moor was told to get dressed, but not his boots. Pieshop told me to have an arrow ready. The Moor led us up a hill covered with trees. We had no idea if we were walking into a trap. The whole of the French army could be camped over the next hill. Vic told us that the Moor had found the old man next to these giant horned beasts and thought he was asleep. When he realised Arthur was dead, he had simply taken what he needed.

We came out of the woods and continued over more meadows. I took some of Icky's mushrooms. When we got to the top of another hill I looked across the landscape. There was a large valley with patches of meadow all around. At the bottom of the valley was a large lake. We started to make our way through fields of wheat. Parts of it were so steep I couldn't stop coming down. I heard a bell ring and turned to fire. Nearby were the two largest Ox's I have ever seen. Their horns must have been about three feet long. They stood, one looking one way, the other looking the other way.

'They could be Auroch Bulls,' said Vic. 'I have not seen one this far West. Usually, they are found in the East or in Northern Europe, in places such as…'

He stopped. In-between these two creatures we saw Arthur's feet sticking up from out of the grass. The bulls stepped back slightly as we approached. Arthur looked as if he had merely lain down and fallen asleep. The Moor explained that this was how he had found him. I moved one bull out of the way and checked Arthur. There were no signs of any injury. Around his lips was a thin red line. A piece of cloth nearby had patches of blood. His cough had been worse than we had all thought. I opened his shirt. His amulet was still around his neck. I remained kneeling on the soft grass, and quietly said a Christian prayer for the dead. Vic gave his own expert medical opinion.

'He's colder than a witches tit.'

'Well,' said Derryck. 'Who's going to do it?'

'I don't mind,' I replied.

'Good boy,' said Derryck. 'Good boy. You know it makes sense. Give him a bit of a head start then just fire an arrow into his back.'

I stopped him. 'I thought you was talking about burying Arthur. You were the one who wanted to kill him in the woods.'

Derryck lifted his hand to show he had two fingers crossed. 'I had veinies. Just kill the Moor and we can go home.'

I stood up. 'But the Moor didn't kill Arthur. He died of consumption.' I took off the necklace and asked the Moor why he didn't take this. He told Vic that he thought it was Arthurs religious charm, so left it untouched. The moor got on his knees and began to cry. The two bulls had no idea what was going on and stared at us with a mixture of apathy and sadness.

Pieshop stepped forward and put a hand on the Moor's shoulder. 'Don't worry lad, I've got a better plan; but we are going to have to wait until the north star is out.'

Chapter 27

A day may come when the courage of men fails, when we forsake our friends and break all bonds of fellowship, but it is not this day.
    Aragorn, The Lord of the Rings: Return of the King, J.R.R. TOLKIEN.

We sat on the side of a hill while and waited for night to fall. I hadn't eaten all day, so when Icky offered me some more mushrooms, I took a handful. By now Icky must have had about three bucket loads. A few wooden huts were dotted on the other side of the lake. The Gaul's had probably settled here over a thousand years ago. Vic said the white Druids were here ten thousand years before that. I didn't know the world was that old. The forests had been left untouched because it was too difficult to remove the trees by horse and cart and the land was too steep to farm. The lake was being fed by the rain and snow. The crystal water swirled in blue and green as a local fisherman moored upon a distant shore and took his catch inside. As the sun began dip, it turned each cotton cloud into a blanket of orange and red to signify twilight. I thought it was fitting for Arthur to go in such a place and time, on a chariot of fire in the clouds. Feeling slightly strange, I could picture myself on a boat on a river, with tangerine trees and marmalade skies.

We carried Arthur as close to the lake as possible. The cabins along the far bank blinked faded lamps in forlorn windows. I stood on the edge and watched the ripples change their size and saw my shrunken head looking down on me above. Pieshop told me to take a few steps back.

We crouched in the darkness as Icky joined us.

'Where's Derryck?' Pieshop asked him. 'Has he gone for a dinghy?'

'Yeah' replied Icky. 'Then after he's buried it he said he was going off to get a little boat.'

We waited. I thought the stars were moving. A lonely owl called out from somewhere in the trees. Bats skimmed across the surface of the water. Another figure came towards us. I thought it was a giant.

'Got one,' said Derryck.
Behind him, Vic and the Moor were wading in the water, pulling a long wooden boat as quietly as possible.

'Did you buy it?' Pieshop asked.
Derryck shook his head. 'No, I nicked it.' He nodded at the dead body. 'It's what Arthur would have wanted.'

The long boat gently bobbed in the shallow water. It was a tramp tug, used to carry leather goods and men's things for the weekend. Arthur would have smiled at the boats name, appropriately titled, *La Chatte Pourrie*.

When the valley was in darkness, we loaded Arthur onto the deck. He was placed on his back, the same position he had taken up for most of his working life. He would be looking at the same Northern star that had guided so many of his ancestors in their longships. The horned helmet was put on his head. We kept his shaving blade and wet stone, the bald old git wouldn't need it in Valhalla, said Derryck. Some pitched tar was placed around him. Pieshop said a Christian prayer, then to cover every chance of Arthur reaching the right destination he placed a coin on Arthur's eye lids like the ancient Greeks did to pay for the body to be transported into the underworld. If Arthur did reach the other side, he would have put those coins into his pocket before anyone noticed. I kept his amulet, as I wanted to give it to Rebekah.

The single sail of the narrow boat was slowly raised. We gently pushed the boat out towards the middle of the lake. At first it floated aimlessly without direction, as the only current available was that of the force that we had exerted. Then a gentle wind carried him, and Arthur slowly drifted away from us. What connection had I made with this old man? We had shared moments of laughter, sadness, fear, and joy. I had fallen in love with his beautiful niece, he had fallen in love with a fat pickled onion seller who had been born in Nice. He could have ignored me because I was so young, but he never. Instead, he made the time to pass on his wisdom.

He once told me that his biggest regrets in life were not the things he tried and failed, but the times he didn't try at all. I wondered what regrets I would have if I ever got that old.

Icky stood beside me as our friend moved away in this wooden vessel. Perhaps he too was pondering the nature of existence. Was Icky thinking we were all on a journey that never really ends, coming back in different forms like the sand in an hourglass. Or that our lives were nothing more than a performance, shining for a few brief moments before being blown out with sleep. What wise thoughts were going through my friend's mind as he looked up at the night sky filled with a thousand stars? That all matter is merely energy condensed to a slow vibration, that we are all one consciousness experiencing itself subjectively; there is no such thing as death, life is only a dream, and we are the imagination of ourselves? Icky leaned close in and gently whispered,

'I am off my fucking nut.'

'What were those mushrooms? I whispered back.

Icky smiled, 'Magic.'

The boat reached the middle of the lake. Vic stood on the edge and sang a song. I don't know if it was ancient Celtic, Greek, Norse, or something far deeper. I can only translate part of it: "Life is brief, fall in love, maidens, before the boat drifts away on the waves, before the hand resting on your shoulder becomes frail."

As the moon slowly disappeared behind a grey cloud, I thought I heard a horn being blown in the distance as if in memory of Einar the Viking warrior. Pieshop's son lit a small fire. I picked up my longbow and an arrow that had a rag coated in pitched tar wrapped near the head. We dipped our arrows into the flames then fired them up into the darkness. Mine reached its zenith, dipped, and hit the side of the boat. I fired again. The arrow went high into the air and landed on the deck. The flames glowed a bright blue as the tar caught fire. We repeated the process for the third and last time. The father, the son, and the holy ghost.

Flames from the boat grew bright enough for us to see Arthurs body between the rising smoke. Surrounded by a twilight of red and orange, he was now a true Viking warrior. We stood alone together with the memories of our dead friend.

As the boat began to blaze, a lamp light on the far side of the lake appeared. Shouting. Then more lights. People came out in their night clothes. They began shouting at each other. The flames caught the mast and sail as smoke bellowed towards the stars. The boat began to dip. Wood cracked and hissed as the hull slipped into the depths. Arthur had become earth, air, fire, and water all at once. It was what he always wanted.

'We'd best be off,' said Pieshop as the crowd looked for who had started the fire. The dark-skinned Moor finally spoke in a language we understood.

'You English,' he said as we walked away. 'You all fucking crazy.'

Pieshop handed him back his pouch and told him he was free to go. We paced silently back up the hill. When we reached the top, we looked back down at the lake. The burning boat had gone, the old thief was no more. A figure appeared between the two bulls.

'Wait,' said the Moor. 'Can I join you?'

PART 4

DAY OF DAYS

Chapter 28

Men wanted for hazardous journey. Low wages, bitter cold, long hours of complete darkness. Safe return doubtful. Honour and recognition in event of success.

    Ernest Shakleton's advert in a national newspaper for men to join him on a journey to the Antarctic at the start of 1914. Over ten thousand English men applied.

We travelled back towards Harfleur. A local woman was surprised we had a dark-skinned Moor with us. She asked if the fort had surrendered. Yes. We asked if she had seen the French army? She shrugged, hoping to get on with her life. At least there was no more sounds of cannon fire to upset her goose. We thought about Arthur. Derryck mentioned that Arthur was not the sharpest quill in the inkwell. Even his wisdom teeth had left him out of boredom. Rebekah reckoned Arthur had always had health issues. He had been a heavy drinker since the age of nine, and now the poor sod ended up buried in water. I think he would have laughed at the irony.

    When we got to the camp the soldiers were shocked to see the Moor. With no black people in England, many soldiers thought he was a bad omen. Vic pointed out we had only met the Moor after we had taken the fort. He wasn't a French spy; he was a sailor. We went into general Bates tent and asked if the Moor could join us. He shook his head.

    'In the entire history of human conflict, no man has ever turned around and said, "Oh goody, the Muslims have arrived."'

General Bates had a surprise for us. King Henry did not feel that a victory had been accomplished. He wanted a battle, even if he had to cross the Somme river and fight the French army in Paris. We were staying here for the time being.

In the meantime, nearly a thousand men were transported home. Around the camp there another thousand men were ill with dysentery. That left about six thousand. The army would be split into three groups: one set of archers and us under the old baron Thomas Camoys. The foot soldiers to be commanded by the King, and the rest of the archers to be led by Edward, the Duke of York. The plan would be to travel towards Paris and demand part of Normandy to be returned to England. Many of us had joined because we believed the French were going to invade our country. Others believed it was to get back what was rightfully ours. Now we were being told that we were going to be the aggressors. I just wanted to go home.

Working with a physician I knew the truth of what this campaign had cost. Two thousand men had died in two months, nearly all from disease. No doubt they would all be hailed as heroes in the history books. I thought of Rodney. I would tell his mother that her son had fought bravely.

I found Rebekah in a field in with two hundred soldiers laid out like a half-arsed graveyard. Every couple of paces was a hole for them to crap in. Some knights believed that the sick men were shirking, and so leaving them outside without tents was a way of making sure who was really ill. It was the equity of medical politics, the architecture of morality, the abuse of power. Rebekah gave them herbal tea. These same men, who a month ago would grab her and talk loudly about the size of their manhood, were now like small boys under a blanket who wanted their mum.

I don't know why none of us had been inflicted by this virus. Maybe that month of digging cess pits in St. Albans had made us immune. Tony would always try to cook us something fresh (usually with garlic). Rebekah made us drink apple cider vinegar every day. She had not got sick, and she was in the infirmary more than anyone. Maybe she was a witch. When she saw me, she smiled, then her face changed. She knew it was bad news before I had said anything.

I told her everything that had happened. Arthur had been coughing ever since we had been stationed in St. Albans. I think he knew his time was almost up. Under a starry night he went out and sat under the same universe the Vikings had used to navigate their longships home. He had fallen into a dream state and not woken up. We had done our best to make him be at peace in the afterlife. I held her close and gently kissed her forehead as she wept.

I remembered the amulet he wore (had worn. It's hard when they have gone and you can still remember their laugh) and took it out of my pocket.

'He said it was the Skuld's Net. The web of the world that symbolizes all the possibilities that the present, the past, and the future, have on our lives. You should have it.'
She took the necklace and placed it over my head.

'You wear it until we get back home. He liked you. He said you were special.'
Whenever she said *We*, I felt a moment of elation. It was the possibility that the future was more than just a dream. 'I hope Dr Culpepper takes us both on. You as a nurse and me as an apprentice.'

'I can't be too far from Shenley,' Rebekah replied. 'I need to help my mother.'

'The money might not be good.'

'I don't care about the money,' she replied. 'I just want to be with you.'
I decided that I was going to be with Rebekah no matter what. She had a beauty that could save the world. I held her tight. We laughed about Arthur jumping out of the boat wearing his

Viking helmet and getting his beard wet as he tried to run to the shore like a Viking Dwarf. Or the times he would climb out from under a cart and dust himself down. He didn't care. In some ways Arthur not only enjoyed his low status, but he also actively went out of his way to stay there. To him, being working class was a badge of honour, not something to hide from. He always had enough to get by, he enjoyed being among family and friends, and he worked to live, not the other way around. In the end, that was all he wanted, to be happy.

The Moor wanted to stay with us even though he would not get paid. People came from the other camps just to look at him. The Moor said he had been to many ports all over the world, and many brothels. He and Icky became firm friends. General Bates believed the Duke of York might be able to use him as a scout when we marched towards Paris.

'I guess that makes you a Yorkshire Moor,' he said.

It was Icky who comforted Olive with lots of cuddles and sympathy. Within three nights he was banging the pickled onions out of her. For a large woman Icky reckoned she was as small as a jockey's pocket. Icky said it's what Arthur would have wanted. Her English did not improve now that she was with a scouser. Lying awake under my blanket, I would often hear her call out, 'I'm arriving, I'm arriving,' as a puffing Icky pulled into her love shed. Life goes on, I suppose.

We ended up staying in Harfleur for another couple of weeks. Some of the knights shipped themselves back home. Derryck started courting Ophelia on a regular basis now that trade that dipped. Every day there were rumours. The French army were gathering forces. If we don't leave now, we would be trapped by time and tide, our fortunes resting on the weather. If we were going to leave, it had to be soon. If we were going to fight, it had to be sooner. The sick continued to keep dying.

Among the knights who had remained was Sir Michael Tate. The piece of shit had so far avoided anything that could be considered work. On the bright side, it allowed Pieshop to see his son on a regular basis. With his boy beside him, Pieshop helped repair the castle gates. Other soldiers helped the French fishermen bring in the catch and smoke them before the weather turned or helped the French farmers get ready to plant Winter crops.

Tony had a real connection with the animals. He could make any horse plough an extra field. Maybe it was because that whenever his affliction would overcome him, the animals did not leave, nor did they laugh, or become afraid. Quite often they would come closer to make sure he was OK.

By the end of September going home was on most men's minds. Every day in the camp was a step closer to the simple truth, Winter was coming. The French army, perhaps numbering twenty thousand men, were also aware that the last move had yet to be played.

Henry changed plans. We were going home. The knights rattled their swords at shadows in the wind, claiming they were ready to kill a hundred men in battle. The rest of us, those who had seen their brothers take their last breath, were glad it was finally over. The camp began to be dismantled. It was agreed that nearly a thousand men would be left in Harfleur to be sent home. The rest of us, now down to around a few hundred knights, a thousand soldiers, and four thousand archers, would march up the coast and then sail from Calais and Dunkirk. We had to due to the weather and the length of time it would take to organise so many ships.

The one thing that would not leave was the rumour that just like Hannibal and his elephants, the French army had waited and waited and waited until we were too weak and exhausted to fight; and were now lying in wait to pick us off.

The Moor wanted to stay with us until we reached Calais and then get a ship to Cadiz. I expected this dark-skinned pirate, whose eyes and teeth shone like newly opened sails, to have a warrior sobriquet fit for the tribal village he had been born in, something that signified his cultural heritage.

   'My ebony skinned traveller born in the heart of the hottest volcano. The man with exotic hair and who follows strange Gods, what did your Kalahari kin name you?'

   'Barry,' he replied. 'Barry Cheeseman.'

That's the name he had been given when he had sailed into France. And so, it was decreed. Arthur was replaced by Barry. We began to show him the ropes. After that, we showed him the tent poles, the canvasses, and gave him Arthur's shovel. From what English he knew, he told us about travelling the known world. His Elephant Stone was used to guide ships to distant shores. I went to give the stone back to him, but he said it was a gift for saving his life. He knew of plants that I had never heard of, and what they could be used for. In some countries men would burn the hemp plant and inhale the smoke. He showed Icky how to do it. We did not see them for three days. All the strawberry jam in the camp also disappeared.

   Tony was offered to stay in Harfleur to cook for some of the knights before they were shipped home. He refused. Rebekah was also offered to wait in Harfleur and travel back with the sick. Instead, she volunteered to come with us and help anyone who became ill on the journey. I was a bit torn with this. Although we would be together, the rumours of a French army waiting for us never went away.

   We left the town on 8th October, the birthday of Pyrrhus, the man who gave us the phrase "Pyrrhic Victory". It was also the day celebrated by the Catholics as the feast of Saint Simeon. He was the man told by God that he would not die until he had seen the Messiah, and then had to spend the rest of his life waiting (in fear or hope?) until it happened.

It had been nearly two months since we had last seen England. We had left with ten thousand men. And now there were so few of us that Pieshop was able to march alongside his son. A thousand soldiers too sick to move wished us luck. The two thousand dead Englishmen buried in a foreign field remained silent. And the same rumour kept turning and twisting with every step we took. A French army of thirty thousand men were waiting, ready to do battle in whatever field they chose.

Chapter 29

You affect the world by what you browse.
  Tim Berners Lee, inventor of worldwide web.

We moved slowly through the lanes of France, always searching the landscape. The mood was different from the pilgrimage we had made through England. The French people saw us as no different than the Romans. Nearly all of us carried a pair of dead man's boots. I wore the clothes of an archer who a year ago would have towered above me. Three months of shovelling hard soil now meant I could pull the string of my longbow back with ease and shoot at least twenty arrows before my arm grew tired. We did not bother with armour. When they said that if I was caught the French would cut off my fingers, I always replied that if I was stupid enough to let the French catch me, I deserved to lose them.

We were three days out when it was confirmed the French army were heading towards the coast to cut us off. We turned and moved towards Amiens. Then we were told the French army were waiting just outside the town. The knights spoke about the code of chivalry and how we should formally plan a battle. They would say that, wouldn't they. If captured, they would be kept well fed, and a ransom paid for their safe return. We were the lowest of the low. The men who had laboured all their lives to keep the privileged few fed on lamb and wine would be thrown to the lions. Only pity would keep us alive if we were defeated.

We changed direction again. More rumours. The French army had thirty thousand men. Six for every Englishman left. We were low on food, people were still falling sick, and we had three hundred miles to go before we reached Calais. If we missed the tide, we would have to march further north up to Dunkirk. If we were not out by November, we would have to spend the Winter months fighting on the beaches.

We took to marching through forests, no different from the barbarians a thousand years ago. But now we stretched out like a weak stream of piss; barely making a sound, and easily broken. I met an archer who had been captured and had two fingers on their right hand cut off. He said he was lucky. He had heard the French would rub shit into the open wound to infect your whole body.

After we had been marching for over a week. We sat under the canopy of a Yew tree and ate some squirrels with the last of the bread, cheese, and pickled onions. Pieshop gave his son most of his food. The boy was still quite small. He was only twelve and had not had his growth spurt. Pieshop said he took after his mother. It was here we were told the French had blocked every bridge across the river Somme. We were trapped.

The knights wanted to move to a field and request a parley; allowing them to escape any ambush and be able to battle the French Knights on what they called a level playing field. I listened with a mixture of shock and sadness. Pieshop said he would rather fight than surrender. Perhaps it did not matter. Within a couple of weeks, we would have died from starvation.

When we reached the river Somme all the bridges were blocked. Henry turned east, deeper into France. He asked for volunteers to go out and find any part of the river to cross. Barry offered to go, as the French would never mistake him for being English.

'I'm going to go with him,' said Icky.
We were all shocked. As a scouser, Icky held on to his free time the same way most men held their balls. 'Are you sure?'

He shrugged. 'To be honest, I haven't really done much since I've been here. This gives me a chance to say I've done something with my life,' Icky put on his cloak and walked into the woods.

We didn't see them the next day. Rebekah waited with us while we dug a shallow grave. The dead archer had a lot of scars and injuries, but not from any battles. These were from years of working to feed himself and his family. His country had called, and he had answered. I was not sure how he had died. Possibly food poisoning. Men were eating acorns to stop starvation. Rebekah told the men to make sure they had no holes in them and to boil or soak them in a jar for a few hours. We began to kill the horses. The problem was the amount of time it took to carve and cook them. Some men ate the meat raw.

When Barry and Icky returned, they had found a place where the locals had rolled large tree trunks across a part of the riverbed to make it shallow enough to clean the horses and carts. The logs would usually get washed away by the Winter rains. They had been spotted by some soldiers and split up. Icky had been caught. He showed us the two stumps that stuck out from his knuckles and shook his head.

'I'm never going to be able to please the wife again. She used to love it when we went bowling. Just think, the next time I make her smile in bed it will be because I've brought her up breakfast.'

We were shocked. None of us knew he was married. Culpepper gave him some good news and some bad news. It was a clean cut, less chance of infection. But it had not been where the bones joined. Culpepper was going to have to dig out the flesh, snip the pieces of bone off, and then stitch the skin back over to help it heal. And I was going to help him.

Icky drank some wine and gave Barry his dirty book. Tony gave him the last of the hemp cake. Icky was more sad about that more than anything else. I strapped his hand to a block of wood. I found that I did not shirk from my duties. Instead, I was fascinated, and knew I could perform the same operation in the future. Afterwards, Icky was allowed to ride in the back of a cart.

As we walked behind it, I noticed that the side of the road was becoming more and more littered with army equipment with every step. People didn't want to carry tents, pots, pans, and empty jars if they had to make a run for it. At nightfall we waited at the part of the river Somme that the French had failed to guard.

Ropes were tied from one side to the other. Five thousand men waded through the wet river in the dark, along with horses and equipment. The logs below us were loose and slippery. A good rain and they would all be gone. On the other side we shivered, unable to stop and dry ourselves properly. Pieshop was happy. He held his son and said that we few, we happy few, had escaped the French trap and now just had to reach Calais or Dunkirk to get home. I was not so sure.

The French were travelling by road, we were using ancient tracks. They had food, we chewed twigs. They were welcomed by the natives; we were strangers in a strange land. And they knew exactly where we were heading. As we made our way through the woods, the sun began to rise in the East. I knew that it was not the end, it was not even the beginning of the end. It felt as if it was, perhaps, the end of the beginning.

Chapter 30

All the things that I shout about
(But never act upon)
All the courage and the dreams I have
(But seem to wait so long)
My doubt is cast aside
Watch phonies run to hide
The dignified don't even enter in the game.
   The Jam, Beat Surrender.

To cheer Icky up we decided to give him a nickname. He had found a knight's battle axe and wanted to be called "Big Chopper", but we had seen him in the bushes, so that was ruled out. A vote was taken. There was a few contenders: The Dirty Half a dozen, Three-skin, The Midgets barber, all were pretty good. Close second was "Sundial", as they also had only one working hand. But the winner was "Ringo", because whenever he got drunk he would call out, "Where's me ring go?"

After crossing the river, the French people were different. It felt as if it was now them and us. If we wanted something, we had to take it. There was never any notion of violating the women or children. We just wanted food.

Icky's injury slowed us down, leaving us at the back of the line with the knights. The attitude of some of them annoyed us, especially Sir Tate, who refused to get off his horse to let it rest. We then found out they were keeping on to their own food. I wished Arthur was here. He would have stolen most of it.

One day we found a chateau. The owner said that even though we were illegal travellers we were welcome to whatever the serfs on his land could afford to give. The tight bastard was happy to take the moral high ground as long as his workers paid the price. On the way back we passed a duck pond. His rich young son sat writing a poem while the peasants worked.

'Gentlemen,' he asked us. 'Do you know why the stone sinks, and the boat floats?'

'Don't get cunty,' said Vic as he kicked the man into the water. Being an artist himself, Vic Flange was always highly critical of other people's work.
Tony laughed so hard he fell into the reeds and killed a duck, so at least we had something to eat. It was a short moment of happiness in what was feeling like a long solemn retreat.

For the next five days and nights we were chased through the countryside by ghosts of the French army. They killed about thirty men who had wandered off the paths or had got too slow. Having Pieshop's son with us took our mind of things. I don't think he understood the danger we were in. He stayed with us while the knights tried to give orders. It didn't really matter. The French knew exactly where we were heading and were simply waiting for the right time and place to strike.

One night we came to a chateau and demanded all the food and drink from the cellar. Henry complained that an army filled with wine was incapable of making a good decision. We didn't care. We had not had full stomachs in weeks. It was good to eat and drink again. The main difference was that there was not much talking or laughter as when we had been in Harfleur.

I went out to watch the night sky. Storm clouds were coming. Finding a spot on the side of a hill I sat under a tree and stretched out the three lengths of string for my longbow to make sure they were clean of knots.

'Keep it under your hat,' said Pieshop as he sat next to me. We could see the French fires a few miles away. We both knew they were going to have to face them, soon. He tapped the ivory clasp on my longbow. 'I hope that doesn't affect your aim.' I knew what he meant. With so many men dead or sick, the idea of us being safe behind the lines when the battle started was long gone. We would be called to fight. I finally confessed to something that had been on my mind since I first joined up. 'What if I can't kill a man,' I said. 'What if, when the time comes, and I just can't do it?'

'You're ready,' Pieshop replied. 'All this training has got your body ready. When it comes to your mind, you're fighting for England, and home. When it comes to your soul, God forgives every soldier.'

There was something else. Something that had caused me to wonder if my fate was already written in the stars.

'My dad committed suicide. What if God believes I should be punished for his sins?'
I waited for an answer. And then came a moment that has stayed with me all my life.

'I remember your father,' said Pieshop. 'We spent the night on the eve of a different battle talking about our future. My son had just been born. Your father talked about how bright you were, and his dreams of what sort of man you would become. Now the time has come to tell you the truth. Your father didn't kill himself. He went to the docks to sell some old rope. One of the ships that day had come in filled with tapestries. He saw a group of foreign sailors raping a young girl, no more than ten years old. Your father fought all of them and managed to get the girl to escape. The men came after him and pushed him into the water. They held him down until he drowned. It was covered up by a group of wealthy merchants because they believed their trade deal was more important than the life of a low status person. I know this because I was a hired mercenary at the time. I was paid to find the girl. Which I did. Then I realised who had died. They wanted me to kill her. I did not. Instead, I took her home. After watching your father being refused a church funeral and buried in a pauper's grave, I decided I would never kill for money again. It was only my son running away to fight that made me join up. Then I saw you at Hackney Marshes. And now, I find myself on this hill, on the eve of another battle, with you. Perhaps Vic's idea about eternal recurrence may have a ring of truth to it.'

I was stunned. I had so many questions running through my head that I barely knew where to start.

'My dad didn't kill himself?'

Pieshop shook his head. 'He was a good man who died fighting to save a child.'

I had carried this burden around with me for the last few years. The main emotion was shame. Would my life have been different had I of known the truth back then, would I even be here on this night?

'Why are you telling me this now?'

'I believe you are ready.'

Still so many questions. So much had happened since we had first met. 'But you've been there when I've played football, got drunk, been arrested, shovelled shit for a living, got into a fight, took drugs, nicked a boat, and got laid.'

Pieshop placed his hand on my shoulder. 'You're welcome. I know your father would have been proud. Now you are ready to start taking some responsibility for your life.'

My mind kept revolving. 'How well did you know my father?'

'We travelled down to Shrewsbury together. He was someone I was willing to stand side by side with. When he left the army, I stayed on and worked for various people here and abroad. But whenever I was in London, I would seek him out among the church roofs. He was always proud of you; said you were one of the best junior archers in London but wanted you to make something of yourself.'

I tried to remember if I had seen Pieshop when I was a boy, or when they put my father in a paupers grave. All I could think of was my mother holding us, telling us to always look forward no matter what. I was so stupid I just spend the whole looking straight ahead of me. Had Pieshop been there and seen me cry?

I spent the rest of the night asking him about my dad, who were the merchants who covered it up, who paid him, did the girl see him die? I even wanted to know the name of the ship. Pieshop tried to answer as much as he could. As I listened, it was as if a screen had been removed, shadows disappeared, and the blinding truth had been revealed. I had been living in darkness all this time.

It started to rain. I didn't care. I stayed on that hill. My mind was unable to rest. All those years of believing one thing, only to find out it wasn't true. I wondered if I should just accept my suffering in order to find redemption. I looked at the notches on my father's longbow. Fuck redemption. I wanted revenge.

Chapter 31

Better stop dreaming of the quiet life
Cause it's the one we'll never know
And quit running for that runaway bus
Cause those rosy days are few
And stop apologizing for the things you've never done
Cause time is short and life is cruel but it's up to us to change
   THE JAM, Town Called malice.

We had crossed the river. The die had been cast. I had found out the truth about my father. I could never go back. It continued to rain as we marched north. A cold coming we had of it. Perhaps the French army would simply return to their provinces and seek comfort in a warm tavern. I stayed silent, keeping my thoughts. The rain fell with a monotonous languor, wounding my heart with a sickness for home. Derryck stepped into a deep puddle and demanded to know what the fuck we were doing here.

We kept marching, hoping those at the front knew where they were going. Some said that we must be close to the sea as they could smell the salt in the air. Vic said it was probably the farmers ploughing for Winter crops and using seaweed to help put minerals back into the soil. The men preferred the first theory. In desperate times it's easier to believe in false hope than a simple truth.

Another rumour. The French army had marched around our flank and were now blocking the route to Calais. Another rumour, French soldiers had massacred everyone left at Harfleur and were also coming up our rear. Another rumour, thirty thousand French soldiers now stretched all the way between Paris and the coast. Should we surrender and hope they let us go, or stand and fight even if we had no chance of winning? The rain continued to fall as we crept along mile after petty mile.

   Our language changed. It became more tense. Not past tense or present tense, just tense. Fuck became the word of the campaign and added to every sentence. Fuck, fuck it, fuck this, fuck that, fuck you, fuck up, fuck off, fuck yes, fuck no, what the fuck? Then you had fucking, where's the fucking cheese, and everything that goes with that word. Fucked, fucker, fuck-a-doodle-do. There was also the C word. Becky hated me saying that word, so I didn't, but the men used it often, even just to say hello.

   At night we could see the fires from the camps of the French army in the distance. So large in number were they, I realised they could attack us whenever they wanted. We were a lamb to their lions. They must have been waiting to meet us in a field large enough for them to show their strength. If we did not surrender, they wanted our inevitable defeat to look like a battle.

   The ground became a heavy wet clay that seemed to seep into our feet. Mud rose up to our knees. There was shouting somewhere at the front of the line. We stopped in a field that had been used by sheep. It was surrounded by deciduous woodland. Nearby was a large set of fields that had been recently ploughed. Vic picked up a piece of wet clay. The soil was so poor it was probably left fallow all summer and only used for large winter crops. The rain must have been heavy in the last few days. The mud was incredibly wet. We walked through the wood and up to a line of trees.

   There was a large, ploughed field, a couple of acres, rectangular in length. To our left out three quarters of the way up was a small village and an ancient Roman set of ruins. The field was surrounded by woodlands, which acted as drainage to stop the fields from flooding. At the other end of this field the whole of the French army was waiting less than a mile away. They were so large they spread out nearly half a mile wide and a mile back. There must have been thousands of knights, horses, foot soldiers, crossbow regiments, and enough food to last weeks. They had chosen this place because it was the only field big enough for all the knights to be able to parade when we surrendered. It was pointless to dig in and try to turn it into a war of attrition. I heard someone say that the old Roman ruins had given its name to the field. It was not down on any map. Vic said true places never are. Pieshop asked what it was called. An answer came back, Agincourt.

Chapter 32

I have seen the moment of my greatness flicker,
And I have seen the eternal Footman hold my coat,
   and snicker,
And in short, I was afraid.
   T.S. Eliot. The Love Song of Alfred J Prufrock

We sat against a cart trying to keep dry. General Bates came over to us. He was looking for the right words to get volunteers to venture through the woods, travel past the ancient fort, go around to the back of the French camp, get some idea of their plans, and then return.

'I think the phrase you are looking for general,' said Derryck, 'Is suicide mission.'

Before we could say anything else, Barry offered to do it. As there were no black people in England, he would not be suspected of being a spy. He would walk into the French camp pretending to be selling charms. We all started off with the usual. Fuck that. Then after a while I agreed to go with him, fuck it. Then Pieshop, then Derryck, after calling me a lucky little fucker, then all the others. We knew that getting caught would mean our immediate deaths. Icky Fingers requested to go but was declined. He could be positioned at the edge of the English camp to make sure we were not fired on by our own soldiers when returning. Pieshop's son asked to go and was refused. The general then took me and Pieshop to one side. If Barry made any signal that he was about to betray us, we were to kill him.

The English army was keeping itself busy by erecting a camp for the knights and physician's tents a few fields away. King Henry decided that all the food we had left was to be cooked. The fires were hard to light in the rain, but eventually they got going. Although some men compared it to the last supper, hungry bellies soon queued up with their bowls to get their first (and last) decent meal in days. Pieshop said it was a good move. Those who had been unwell might now have the energy to fight the next day. Then he quietly went off to give his son his share.

   I went and checked my arrows. Thicker shafts with goose feathers worked best in the rain. Around us men checked their armour, chatting to strangers and swearing as if they were old friends. Other men sharpened their pikes, wet their swords, and said their prayers. These were all just earthly distractions from the divine countenance of an oncoming battle. I checked the feathers on my arrows again, then pressed my finger on each sharpened tip. More distractions from distractions as I waited for the others.

   We left at twilight. The woods would make it impossible to move quickly without a lamp. Our dark hooded cloaks would act as our armour. We hoped not many French guards would be walking around in this weather. A crossbow bolt sits in a groove. As soon as it gets wet it affects the flight of the bolt, while a longbow arrow is far more reliable.

   The rain fell hard enough to drop leaves from branches. It drowned out the sound of our feet as we moved through the woods. We reached the first clearing. There were perhaps three cottages. No lamps were lit. The locals knew what was coming and the French may have put scouts in the upper rooms. We crouched down as we walked past the empty stables.

   The flooded track was only wide enough for a small cart. The woods either side were filled with coppice trees. Vic pressed a foot into the mud. The ground had too much clay in it to soak up all this water. He was glad we did not have any armour. Metal ships would sink. Ahead of us lay the ancient ruins of Agincourt. I could make out a collapsed tower, stone arches, and walls that had fallen over time. It had probably been a sentry post for the Romans on their way to invade England. We crept towards the first wall. No scouts. Perhaps the French army, believing in their own might and the weather, did not feel the need to protect their camp.

We walked on a path tread by the Romans a thousand years ago. Standing on the high ground we looked upon the works of the mighty French empire, and despaired. Stretched into the distance were thousands of French soldiers. A vast landscape of tents, lit by many fires that glistened like a sleeping dragon. The French had been on the road for less than two weeks. They were clean and well supplied with food. At least six fields had been taken over with horses. There were even the large horse breeds used for jousting. In other fields I could see hundreds of tents with flags showing the knights Coat of Arms. Perhaps we've really fucked up here.

'How many do you think there are?' Derryck asked. Pieshop tried to round off the numbers of horses and flags and tents. 'I reckon about thirty thousand.'

'Fuck my old boots,' Derryck replied. 'Theres five thousand of us. That means we've got to kill at least six men each. Terrific.'

Avoiding the slippery mud, we crept towards their camp.

The single track was littered with deep puddles. We moved in an arrow shaped formation, with Vic at the front, and the rest of us fanning out into the woods on either side. Every so often Vic would stop, crouch down, and listen to the sounds of French shouting and laughter. Our eyes remained fixed on the distance for any signs of danger. The closer we got to the French encampment the more we realised they did not seem bothered. They really did expect us to surrender.

Standing about three trees back we could see into the French camp. The knights had positioned themselves at the middle, but had left a large gap to get to the field first. They all wanted to be seen when King Henry would be forced to ride up and surrender. Pieshop said the foot soldiers were so far behind the knights' tents that they would have to walk another half a mile just to get to the battle. The crossbow regiments were placed even further back. The French were treating this more like a war game than a real battle. Barry stepped forward and walked into the French camp as if about to sell them trinkets.

'Allo my friends,' he said to the nearest group of men. 'Looky, looky, looky. You want tell the time?' He showed them small wooden sundials inside his cloak. 'You want fun time?' He showed them various herbs. 'I have Spanish salt, garlic powder, elderberries, something for the weekend.' The men waved him away. He moved further into the camp, giving the same spiel. No seemed that bothered. Within moments we lost sight of him. Derryck was crouching down near me.

'That story about three hundred Spartans, how did they manage to hold the line?'
I kept an eye on Barry. 'They fought at the narrowest point in the field of battle, which meant the enemy could only put a few men into the front line at a time.'
Derryck thought for a moment. 'So, all these Spartans went back home?'
I shook my head. 'No, someone grassed to the Persian King that there was a secret path. They went around the back and brutally murdered every single Spartan.'
Derryck kept his head down. 'And we've just sent someone into the French camp who knows the layout of our camp. Te-fucking-rific.'

The smell of a hog roasting wafted into to the trees. Tony looked on with jealous admiration as two men turned the greasy beast over a fire. An empty barrel of wine was broken and thrown into the flames. Men cheered and laughed in the rain. We ducked down as soldiers would walk over to take a piss and then rejoin their friends. Pieshop took out his knife and watched one drunk stagger up to the line of trees. He closed his eyes and waved his willy from side to side as he urinated. Once finished, he shook it without any real purpose then turned and called out to his pals that he was off to get more wine. Many of the soldiers were celebrating early. I felt the rain going through my cloak and onto my skin. The string on my longbow was soaking wet.

We waited. Where the fuck was Barry? Finally, he appeared. He was singing to himself as if he was the son and heir of nothing in particular while the armed soldiers pretended they didn't see him. What the fuck had he been doing all this time? Just before he got to us, a Frenchman came running after him. We ducked back down. The Frenchman had a handful of animal fat in one hand. He whispered something to Barry, and then with the other hand seemed to offer him money. Barry shook his head. The man tried again. Barry quickly ushered him away. The man flicked the grease from his hand, gestured to Barry, and went back to the camp. Barry stepped into the woods, moved forward a few paces, turned, and made his way through the trees that seemed to shiver as the rain bounced off every branch. After a few steps he stopped. Finally, a whisper came through the darkness.

'Is it safe?' Vic asked.

The rain began to fall harder. I wished it would stop and let the men continue their drinking. Better to face a hungover horseman in the morning than a sober soldier. Barry smiled.

'Don't worry. They could not hit an elephant…'

A bolt struck him in the thigh. Barry dropped to the ground. A soldier came down the track carrying a crossbow. He took out another bolt and got ready to fire again. On the other side I could see Pieshop waving at me. The man reached Barry. I had to fire. I came from behind the tree. The man turned to call out to warn the camp. The arrow went into the back of his neck and out of his throat. He seemed to spend a moment transfixed in space before slowly falling forward. We went onto the track to get Barry. Tony picked up the crossbow and some bolts.

'You stopped him from calling out. That has to be the greatest shot I've ever seen.'
I shook my head. 'Not really, I was aiming for his chest.'

As we lifted Barry up, we heard voices coming from the camp. Four soldiers came towards us. Two with crossbows, two with swords. They found their comrade.

'C'est un piège.'

A bolt shot through the woods. We moved towards the fort. The men were shouting for reinforcements. One of the crossbow men bent down to reload. I placed an arrow in my hand. Derryck stepped down beside me. He pulled back his bow and fired. His arrow hit the man with the sword. He was not in full armour. It went into his body, but he did not go down. He went to call out again but got no further when the arrow fired by Pieshop hit him squarely in the chest.

'Get the other one.'
I fired at the man kneeling down. He dived into a puddle. I missed. We grabbed Barry and continued moving. He kept saying something. Vic checked the blood soaked trousers.

'Don't worry Barry. You've still got all your berries.'

We stopped when we reached the ancient fort. Barry was placed on a low wall. Pieshop said that the French probably think we are a band of outlaws and would go back to their camp to set up an armed perimeter rather than chase us. We just had to be careful. I felt mightily relieved. As I stepped through a ruined archway, Pieshop raised his forearm, the rain bouncing off his hand so hard I could hear the skin snapping. He turned to us.

'It's in the trees. It's coming.'

A French knight on horseback appeared out of the woods. He jumped over a fallen trunk and swung his sword at Pieshop, who ducked and fell to the ground. Men came running towards us. The horse jumped over the broken wall, spurted forward and turned to face my friends. My arrow slipped in my hands as the rain kept falling. Another soldier came out from the darkness and landed on Pieshop. He pressed his dagger towards Pieshop's neck. Derryck stopped a soldier who came out of the trees. Both men took out their knives. Another soldier appeared. This one had a crossbow. He bent down and aimed it at Deryck. I stepped around and fired. My arrow went into his chest. I got another arrow and went to fire again. Tony ran over to where Pieshop was fighting and kicked the soldier hard in the side of his stomach. He rolled over as Pieshop pushed him away.

Tony called to Pieshop. 'That should slow him down for a bit.' Tony gave a swift jerk. The bolt left his crossbow and impaled itself deep into the soldier's groin. 'Oh, shit.'

The knight on horseback was heading towards Vic and Barry. Pieshop grabbed his longbow and quickly fired at the horse. The arrow landed, but the shot had been weak. The knight decided he was not going to face a group of archers on his own and steered his horse into the trees. As Derryck and another soldier jabbed and parried with their knives, Vic ran over and stabbed the French soldier in the leg. The soldier fell. Another soldier ran out from behind an ancient wall. He placed his sword at Pieshop's chest. He said something, then went to push the sword into the heart. His head jerked. Behind him, Barry had pulled the crossbow bolt from out of his leg, ran over, and pushed it into the side of the soldier's neck. The soldier dropped the sword as he choked on his own blood. He collapsed the same moment as Barry. Pieshop picked up Barry and put him over his shoulders.

We moved as quickly as we could. Keeping to the trees, afraid to use the path. The rain blew in at an angle, forcing us to keep our heads down. The total darkness gave us no sign of where we were stepping. I could only see three feet in front of me. Barry's leg hung off Pieshop's back. Every jolt caused him to wince, but he stayed silent.

Eventually, we saw the little lights of the English camp. Icky was hiding in the bushes. This time he had kept his trousers on. He saw us and called out. The guards let us through. We did not stop until we found Dr Culpepper's tent. A knight demanded we wait until the king had spoken to us.

I collapsed onto the wet ground. I had taken the life of another man. My first killing would remain with me like a splinter in the mind's eye. I reasoned that if I had not, I would be dead. My hands were shaking in the rain. I looked at my friends. We had made it. Derryck passed around a bottle of wine. Tony admired the crossbow and bolts he had recently gotten.

'It's a shame Arthur's not here,' said Vic.

'Why?'

'Because he'd be climbing out from under that cart and dusting himself down by now.'

We had fought against drunken soldiers and managed to escape. Tomorrow was going to be a sober reckoning. I didn't know any Viking oaths, but a Roman one came to mind. "We who are about to die salute you."

Chapter 33

A Mars a day helps you work rest and play.
    Advert.

Culpepper called me into the tent to help. Icky followed. Barry lay on the operating table, naked from the waist down.
  'It's a big one,' said the doctor.
Icky raised an eyebrow.
  'Well, yes. He's certainly been very lucky.'
Culpepper nodded. 'The other is about the same size.'
Icky gasped. 'He's got two of those?'
Culpepper got Barry to lie on his side and pointed at the exit wound. 'What do you recommend?'
I tried to remember my medical training. 'They are too big to cauterize. To stem the blood, I would put a cold compress of honey and garlic over both wounds, cover them with cabbage leaves, wrap tightly, and give him some cloves to take away the pain. After a few days I would recommend maggots to clean the wounds and then repeat.'
Dr Culpepper concurred with my diagnosis, and we started to work. Barry refused alcohol. He took out a sausage shaped dark lump from his pouch. 'It's hashish,' he told Icky. 'It's good.' He took a bite.
  'I thought it was a sex toy,' Icky replied. 'Like a Moroccan arse tickler.' He took a gobble from the other end.
Barry waited a while. 'It is that as well.'
  A knight came in.

'I say, I do believe this tent has been reserved for a select few. Does that black man even know how to spell infirmary?' Culpepper shook his head. 'No. Tell me, do you know how to spell bugger off?' He pushed him out of the way as we mixed the medicine together. Then we started to treat the wound, Barry let out a scream.

'Could be worse,' said Dr Culpepper.

'How could it be any worse?' Icky asked. 'He's got two bloody big holes in him.'

'The tent next door has got an operating table with a wobbly leg,' Culpepper replied.

Once we had finished I went outside. King Henry was wearing an old cloak in case of assassins. He looked at us, noting that we were all covered in mud.

'What did you see, what did you hear?'

Vic explained that Barry had told him the French felt they were so large and powerful, and we were so small and weak, they were simply going to cook a large breakfast then wait throughout the day for us to surrender. They had plenty of food, while we were starving. They were fresh, while we were all tired. They had plenty of time, while we only had a matter of weeks before the channel would be too rough to cross. They could remain in their camp, while we had to march around them to escape. They had thirty thousand men, and they knew there was less than six thousand of us. The French were so confident they had put their infantry half a mile behind the line, and had only chosen these fields because it could fit the whole of their cavalry even though there was no room for them to go through the woods to try and outflank us. No one seemed interested in our archers. First because they felt the English would surrender after the initial attack, and second because the archers were lowly Englishmen who would run away when faced with such majestic power.

The King stood in a sombre moment of reflection as the rain drummed on the tents and fired off the branches.

'How can I get my men to fight thirty thousand soldiers once the cold light of day reveals how weak we are?'

Pieshop stepped forward. 'Englishmen may fight for their faith, for money, and even their friends, your majesty; but there is one thing they place above all others, hope. Give us hope that if we win we will return home to England. Even if the odds are against us, we will stand our ground.'

'It's a shame you do not have a plan to beat the French.' Pieshop held on to his longbow. 'A man once told me the story of how he captured a powerful lion by letting the creature think it had already won. By the time it realised it had walked into a trap it was too late.'

Pieshop drew a layout of the area in the mud. The fields were the shape of an hourglass, with the French at the top, us at the bottom, and woods on either side. Only so many grains of sand can go through at its narrowest point, and it is the same with soldiers. The soil was heavy clay. It had recently been ploughed. The heavy rain would make it feel as though every step was walking into a series of buckets. The French did not expect to fight in the wet mud. They expected us to surrender. The best place for their English to make a stand would be just below the narrowest point in the fields, with the French line about six hundred yards away. This would make them out of range for our longbows, and us out of range for their crossbows. But we had the advantage because our killing distance was further than theirs. As soon as they started moving down the field, they would have to bunch closer and closer together, churning up the wet mud, causing them to slow down. We would then be able to land the first blows. The king almost agreed.

'There is of course, one fatal flaw in this plan. We have to get them to attack first. Why on earth would they do that?'
Tony then asked to speak to the King.

A short time later the King came back. He called to one of his knights and told them to organise a group of men to get as many tent poles as they could and to turn them into sharpened stakes. Before he walked away, Pieshop called out. 'Your majesty, the Moor did well tonight. He may have saved all our lives.'

'You don't see him as a spy?' The King asked.
Pieshop shook his head. 'No. I see him as my friend.'

We headed back towards our tent. I could see men sat lost in their own thoughts. Some tried to sleep. Others checked their weapons again, and their armour. With some dry wood from inside the tent we got a fire going. Tony brewed the last of the elderberry tea. After a few sips to try and get warm, Pieshop was the first to speak.

'I hope the men we killed tonight get a decent burial. They were soldiers once, and young.'

'You ever killed a man before?' Derryck asked.

'As a soldier?' Pieshop sipped his tea. 'In 1383 I was sixteen years old. The call came to stop the Muslim invasion. They had murdered so many Christian women and children I felt it was my duty to fight. The original crusades were heroic, but Henry Despencers crusade was purely political. We sailed to Calais, through a place called Ypres, and into the fields of Flanders. We set up our siege engines, ready to fight, then the town quickly surrendered. Turns out Despencer was just like all the other politicians…'

'Greedy,' said Derryck.

'Mad,' said Vic.

Tony raised his hands as if in the classroom. 'Cunts?'

Pieshop shook his head. 'Corrupt. Despenser went behind our backs, did a deal with the European noblemen, and left us to fend for ourselves. Myself, and those who still believed in the tradition of the Templars, travelled down to Jerusalem. We found a group of Muslims were destroying a church. We stopped them. Then we travelled back through the ottoman empire.

'When I returned to England I fought in the battle of Shrewsbury. After that I worked as a mercenary. I had no issues with taking a life. One day I heard the voice of God. He told me that a soldier does not kill civilians. I became a carpenter.' Derryck sat and thought about what he had just heard and felt the need to ask another question.

'So, how many men have you killed, in total?'
Pieshop shrugged. 'I lost count at a hundred.'
Derryck spat out his tea. 'A hundred. Fuck me. You're not a person, you're a plague.'

'I wish I had not killed any of them,' Pieshop replied. 'But there is a brutal truth that all of your religions, politics, poetry and philosophies put together have never understood. You cannot fight back if you are weak or dead. Sometimes you have to strike first if you really believe there is no other choice.' He glanced at me. 'Before the battle starts, think of where you want to be in the future, and aim to get there, no matter who or what stands in your way.'

'London,' said Derryck. 'That's where I want to be. The people are the best in the world. You can't whack the east end for its hospitality, and the food. Although the traffic can be a bit bad if you get stuck behind a slow horse and cart.'
Vic thought for a moment. 'There is a little village in the west called Glastonbury. It has an abbey, and there is also a hill. To sit there on a summer night and play music is where I want to be.'

The favourite place that I could think of was under a blanket with Rebekah. Just a five-minute cuddle was enough to make me feel good. If I survived one more day, I hoped to spend eternity with her in my arms. Tony spoke next.

I don't know what the future holds,' he said. 'So, right now, I'm happy to be here with you lot. And if anyone wants to invade England, they will have to get past me first.'

'And me,' said Vic. 'I'll be standing right beside you Tony.'

'And me,' said Pieshop.

'And me,' said Derryck. 'Although if you start wobbling I'm going to take a step sideways.'

'And meeee,' said Icky, as he ran past, now stark bollock naked, with tribal marks on his face and bandages on his right hand. He ran into the woods. 'Weeee.'
That hashish must be some good shit.

General Bates came over. We were to be among the front-line archers because they were so little in number. With my medical training I would also be exempt if I wanted to. I refused. If I was going to die, I wanted to be with my friends.

'Are we really going to take on thirty thousand French soldiers?' Tony sat perfectly still. The general nodded, then walked away. Tony laughed as he held out a steady hand. 'I can't fucking believe it. I should be shaking like a shitting dog.'

We finished our tea. The mood was now one of final resolution. We few Englishmen were ready to fight a giant foreign beast. Better to be a band of bastards who stood alone together than sheep who weakly surrendered to the mob. I felt the pendant that hung around my neck. Arthur said it was the symbol of how the past, the present and the future, was all interlinked. Perhaps that was also true of England. What did the English at home think of all this, did they know what was happening, and how would we be remembered in the future? I put the cloak hood over my head and waited for the dawn to come.

Chapter 34

From this day to the ending of the world,
We in it shall be remembered-
We few, we happy few, we band of brothers;
For he today that sheds his blood with me
Shall be my brother.

The weak glow from a rising sun dappled off the grey clouds to our right signalled the day was about to begin. The rain finally stopped just before dawn. A blanket of mist swam around our feet. The French were expecting us to surrender. King Henry took one last look and told the Knights to take the horses back to the camp and be prepared for hand-to-hand combat. At that point we knew we were going to fight.

Two riders were approaching. As per the rules of chivalry, all messengers were exempt from being captured, tortured, or killed. They carried a series of banners to signify who the message was from, including that of Charles D'Albret, the man leading the French army. The messenger was dressed in fine clothes, but the trot across the mist covered muddy fields had left his legs covered in clay. The messenger informed Henry that although there was still no word from King Charles in Paris, General D'Albret was willing to take Henry's surrender. The knights would pay a ransom, all weapons and horses taken, with just one horse to ride, and that would be yours. There was no mention as to what would happen to us. Henry thought for a moment, then gave his reply.

'Send a message back to the general.' He raised two fingers. 'Up yours.'

Vic, standing next to me, gave a little laugh. 'I bet that gets changed if the history if this battle is ever written.'

The messenger looked around. 'Your majesty. I have been sent to get your agreement to surrender, which would be signed after morning prayers. If I may be allowed to speak my own words without fear or favour.' He waited for the King to nod, then continued. 'There are thirty thousand French men at the top of those fields, and another six thousand soldiers due to arrive here within the next few days. I can go back and tell the generals that you wish to say morning prayers for Saints Crispin's and speak to your knights before you reach a decision, and that I shall come back for your answer later, if you wish.'

Henry thought for a moment. 'I and my brothers around me, will celebrate Saints Crispin's day here in this field, and those back home will curse the fact they are not with us. We will then decide our own fate, not those who wish to destroy England.'

The messenger knew that this was not the answer that the generals would want to hear. They would demand many times over what exactly was said. Then no doubt he would be told to ride down to the English encampment again. He bowed, and the men rode away. But this time, rather than straight across the fields, they went off into the woods and took his horse along the track, avoiding the puddles.

The foot soldiers were ordered to line up three hundred men wide and wait at the bottom of the field. The duke of York and baron Camoys were to take their archers to the middle of the field and fan out at either side so that the formation was shaped like a V. The tents were lifted to reveal a thousand sharp wooden spikes, and two pieces of wood tied to make an X shape. These were to be put into the ground behind the first line of archers, out of sight of the French.

Pieshop said goodbye to his son and told him to stay in the camp. Men gathered their stakes, shovels, longbows, and arrows. The mud clogged to our boots as we walked up the left side of a mist covered field. The men behind us kept their wooden stakes hidden. We stopped around a thousand yards from the French lines and formed a V shape.

  A thousand French knights, all with the same look of surprise and shock, wondered what we were doing. To be honest, so did I. There were four thousand archers in the middle of the field, and a thousand foot soldiers further back. The woods would protect our flanks, but any breaks in the line and it would surely be all over bar the shouting. We got ready to say our prayers.

  'Pray to God,' said Pieshop. 'Not Jesus. When the battle starts this will be no place for a boy.'
We bent down and kissed the ground to bless the earth. Derryck coughed.

  'For fucks sake. I think I've just swallowed some cow shit.'
We were the front line. We were to fire at least three arrows as the horses approached. Then we would move back behind the stakes to let the professional archer's fire. Another line would take over after that, then it would rotate back to us. That was the plan. But even the best laid plans do not survive first contact. I could feel the water seeping into my boots.

  We had no idea how long the battle was going to last, or what the French would do. I had thirty arrows in my pouch. What happened after they had gone; I did not know.

   A voice was calling out somewhere behind us. Icky appeared (dressed) carrying a battle-axe. Barry was next to him, holding a spike. Tony hugged his friends. Derryck looked at the battle-axe. 'Do you know how to use that?'

  'It's not the first time I've had a large weapon in my hands Del boy.'

'Oh, you helped Barry get dressed. Well, it's good to have you both here. Could be a nice day for it.' We all looked up at the top of the field.

The French had been watching us while enjoying their breakfast. The fires had been burning all night even with the rain, and now the men were cooking fresh meat. They still believed we were going to surrender. They saw our lining up in formation as a way of getting the King to parley.

The messenger rode into view. A few French knights rode out beside him, demanding to know what was going on, no doubt all filled with piss and wind. They seemed to be barking orders. Trumpets sounded. Then the first line cavalry came to the top of the field. They kept coming, and coming, and coming. They wanted to show us just how big and powerful they were. Tony started to laugh. He said he was thinking about that day with little Lord Farquar and the horse. We all started laughing. Those around us wondered if we had gone mad with fear.

As the mist began to clear, I noticed the French knights were not carrying lances. They either were not ready to fight or expected us to flee as soon as the charge started and would use their swords to knock us down. I must admit, seeing them was a wonderous sight. The front line of the cavalry must have measured a thousand horses. Behind them more knights waited for room to mount. The foot soldiers and crossbow battalions must have been so far back they had no idea what was going on. The knights were laughing as they looked down on us. And then something happened that neither they nor I were expecting.

From the trees on either side about two hundred yards from the French line, a small deployment of English archers appeared. They fired into the French cavalry. They were too far away to be able to pierce any armour, but some of the knights fell off their horses, and some of the horses were hit, which made them extremely agitated. The English archers then did something even more unexpected. They raised the two fingers of their right hand to show that they had the capability of firing at them all day. Goading the French even further, they turned around and exposed their buttocks, laughing at these men of nobility.

The band of English archers fired again and ran back into the woods. They hollered as if they were on a hunt. A few horses jolted away. The French noblemen seemed more aggrieved at being insulted by commoners than being fired at. The young Knights became more eager to enter the fray. All of them edging closer and closer towards us, and further away from their commanders. One knight, furious at being treated with such contempt by the plebs, decided he would not wait for a surrender. Nor did he consult with anyone about a change of plans. He started to charge. Other knights followed, each one demanding that their banners reach the English line first.

The French commanders were still waiting to get on their horses. Seeing movement, the drummers rolled the signal for a cavalry charge straight down the field. But the French had made one crucial error. For the last three days it had been pissing down with rain. Believing we were going to surrender, no one had tried to ride a horse carrying a fully armoured Knight over a soaking wet ploughed muddy field. Soon I could see some horses moving away from the French line. The most eager going straight into a full gallop.

At first it all seemed slightly unreal. The mist made it seem as though the knights were riding on clouds. We waited in front of the stakes. Pieshop stood next to me. The horses were coming straight towards us. Those to our left flank were having to move closer together as the field narrowed. Although I knew nothing about horses, it soon became clear to me the mud was far worse than what anyone had expected. The hooves of those first horses churned up the ground, making it harder and harder for the horses behind to keep pace. Other horses struggled with the deep furrows. One or two even fell, causing the horses behind them to trip. But I cannot deny they were certainly a sight of wonder.

'Fuck me,' said Derryck, 'We are going to get absolutely mullered.'

The sound was that of being trapped inside an enormous hourglass as clumps of clay twisted and span in all directions.

'Aim for the horses,' said Pieshop.

Tony held onto his newly obtained crossbow, 'That's a bit out of order.' He shook slightly. A bolt fired out and hit a rabbit. 'Oh, fuck it.'

General Bates rode up behind us.

'Use your worse arrow and let them know we are here.'

On the command, four thousand arrows rose into the grey morning clouds, darkening the landscape. The volley moved as two giant swarms. There was a terrible beauty to their intention. I watched as the first arrows began to dip. They landed on the knights in a hail of metal and wood. Horses fell, along with a few bodies, but not enough to stop the charge. What it did do was cause the knights to pull their visors down as low as they could, effectively making them blind from everything apart from what was directly in front of them. The horses that fell caused at least three other horses to crash behind it. But the cavalry charge kept coming. And they were getting closer.

The ground shook as they approached the three-hundred-yard mark. A wave of destruction would soon drown us. Pieshop called out above the thunder of hooves.

'You may believe that God has planned for you to die today. You may even believe that God will turn the enemy away and you will live for a hundred years. It doesn't matter. God has already given you the greatest gift of being born an English man. That means you don't run. YOU DON'T FUCKING RUN.'

The first wave of the horses came crashing into the killing zone. The riders must have sat twelve feet high. I could see the horse's breath as they strained to reach us. We got the call.

'Fire.'

Chapter 35

A volley of arrows fired directly out from a solid line of English men. Hundreds of horses buckled, fell, turned, or stopped and reared. The horses behind slammed into the wounded animals and trampled over their riders. Knights thrown to the ground were quickly stomped into the ever-sucking mud by a hundred hooves. Injured horses veered sharply towards the centre of the field, then turned back towards a new line of knights who were riding towards us. More knights kept coming. Two hundred yards. Now we aimed at the men.

'Get ready'.

We pulled our strings back as far as we could, every muscle straining to go. The charge became louder.

'Take aim.'

I picked out a knight.

'Fire.'

My arrow went into the breast plate. The rider stayed on his horse, then fell as the knight behind crashed into him. Around them hundreds of horses pulled up or tried to turn, only to be hit by the horses behind them. Once man or beast had fallen into the mud it was impossible for them to get back up. Other knights at the back of the line, who had kept their visors and heads down, continued charging. The cavalry was less than a hundred and fifty yards away. The general called out above the screams.

'Unleash hell.'

I fired at a knight. He was dead before he fell into the mud. His horse was hit by an arrow and charged back towards the French. I got another arrow and pulled back the string. I could feel it take the whole two hundred pounds of pressure. The muscles in my arm found a greater strength than it had ever had before. A knight raised his visor. The arrow hit him in the face. Another knight tried to jump over a dead horse. I knew I could not miss. I fired, and he fell between two horses. More wounded horses turned towards the centre of the field and ran away from the arrows by running straight into their oncoming cavalry charge. I fired again.

'Get back, get back.'

We ran behind the stakes. The knights that were left were less than a hundred yards away. They saw what awaited them and tried to stop.

Now every arrow, whether aimed at man or horse, was a kill shot. The knights could not turn into the woods, and the centre was a quagmire. Those that pulled up were easily picked off. So many wounded horses were now running loose on the field of battle they churned up the mud until it became a bog. They trampled over the bodies of fallen knights, pushing them into the wet mud, their heavy armour leaving them unable to get up. In some ways they were lucky. The second line of riders, their horses weary after trying to get through the mud, were also in range.

Many of the horse became impaled. The blood would burst around us as the knight fell forward. Icky hit one on the back of the head, others soon joined in. This became an easier way of dispatching the enemy. Knights further back were dismounting and calling for our own knights to do battle. Quite often they were silenced by an arrow at short range or a sword in the back. we could see a battalion of French foot soldiers moving down the field.

We were told to move further back behind the spikes. Our ground was still fairly solid. But it meant the French horses had even further to travel in the mud. I saw one that sank so deep all four legs disappeared. It was my turn to fire again. I confess I did not think to consider there were human beings behind the masks. I fired because a thousand-foot soldiers were coming down the field. I let fly five arrows, all hitting their target. The number of French wounded or dead were so high in number the enemy had to climb over them to get to us.

The regiment of French foot soldiers were still coming down the middle of the field. Their journey was made difficult by the mud. Each man must have had an extra thirty pounds of armour attached to them. We adapted our plans. Those who could fire that far were told to aim for the foot soldiers. Another volley. The foot soldiers put down their visors and grouped closer together. They never saw the wounded horses charging towards them. The horses, trained in French war games similar to ours, would take out four or five men at a time. There must have been at least a thousand dead horses on the field, and another two thousand running loose.

The last horses to come forward were the big Destriers. Although better suited to make it through the churned mud, they still had to clamber over dead horses and the bodies of men drowning inside their armour. None of them could get through the yards of wooden stakes. The French knights who had dismounted were now walking towards us with sword and shield in their hands. But out biggest fear was that the French foot soldiers were getting closer and closer to our own soldiers, and our King.

Those who still had arrows left were told to move down the line towards the centre. I could see two regiments coming towards us. The first regiment had churned up the ground so much that a man could sink down past his ankles. The clay stuck to their armoured boots. They soon lost formation. The soldiers, scared about getting hit, kept their heads down, which meant they could not see the horses. Neither could they see us. Our cloth tunics and leather boots meant we did not sink. We bent down, turned our longbows at an angle, and aimed low. If hit in the legs, the men would fall, and have a hundred men walk over them until they were crushed or drowned in the mud.

A few archers broke from the ranks. They stood in front of our line of foot soldiers and fired directly into the French from about three hundred yards. When the first soldier went down, it made every soldier behind him climb over a body to get to us. More archers joined in. As the French got closer, every arrow fired could not miss. At least a thousand men were killed this way. But still they kept coming. Eventually they reached our line and engaged in combat.

I realised I had fired all my arrows. How many I had wounded or killed I did not know. I couldn't understand why the cavalry or army had not been given the call to retreat and regroup. I looked up to see the next battalion of French soldiers marching across the mud. By now it was a quagmire, filled with the bodies of dead horses and drowning men. They had also entered the kill zone. Archers had taken to hiding in the trees and firing at will. Others were engaged in hand-to-hand combat. The French horses were taking out just as many men as us. The noise of the hooves and the shouts and the drums drowned in my ears. As I turned to go back, a wounded horse crashed into me.

I was flung twisting and turning into the wet mud, my head span around and around. It was only as I tried to move that I felt a hand around my neck. A French knight was lying next to me. A steel glove was pushing me down as the knight tried to grab his side dagger. The ground shaking with heavy thuds. I struggled to break free. Lights flashed across my eyes. I looked over to see another injured horse coming directly towards us. Voices were shouting all around me. Encore une fois, Encore une fois. Lights flashed in front of my eyes. The horse was galloping towards us.

I slipped the ivory clasp off my longbow and pushed it into the knight's visor. Using my palm, I slammed the ivory into his eye. He moved backwards. I kicked him away, directly into the feet of the horse. He was churned into the mud. I reached over and took back the clasp.

In the middle of the field King Henry brought another tactic into play. He ordered his foot soldiers to retreat thirty yards, stop, and then hold the line. The first French regiment had to climb over more bodies, and sink into more mud, to fight again. As they engaged in combat, the second French regiment arrived. They could do nothing but wait as arrows hit them from both sides. Only for Henry to order the English into another retreat for thirty yards to the narrowest point in the field, then stand and fight. The French had not realised it, but they had moved so far forward, our line of archers was now behind them. With only leather straps for protection on their backs, every arrow was a kill shot. Those at the very back of the French line were dying more quickly than those at the front. Other archers who had run out of arrows were now attacking the exhausted soldiers with any weapon they had. I saw Derryck hit one soldier in the neck with his shovel.

I ran through the woods to collect all the spare arrows I could. It was only when I turned a corner that something made me stop. Four men on horseback were charging towards me. More horses were behind them. A group of French knights were coming away from the English encampment. I jumped behind a fallen tree. They passed at full gallop. I was too insignificant in events happening today to be of any consideration. I got up and ran down to our camp. I stopped again. What I saw still shocks me to this day.

Chapter 36

We've got to have rules and obey them. After all, we're not savages. We're English, and the English are best at everything.
  William Golding, Lord of the Flies.

At first it all seemed staged, as if from one of Kincaid's morality plays or a scene from a tapestry. Although well away from battle, there were bodies lying in the grass among the rows of tents. None were moving. But none were asleep. A man wearing a suit of armour came out of the nearby bushes. It was Sir Michael Tate. When he saw me, he straightened up and looked down the track.

'Where are the others?'

I had no idea what he was talking about. I ignored him and went to move. He placed a hand on my chest. I pushed it away and went into the camp.

I looked at the first body, then the next. They were boys who had enlisted as servants because they were too young to fight. Sir Tate shouted at me again as the women and the walking wounded came out of the surrounding tents. Dr Culpepper saw me. He said that a group of French knights had rode into the camp to steal the Kings crown. They had attacked anyone who had tried to stop them. None of the children had weapons. This had not been a battle; it was an execution. Sir Tate prodded me with his sword. 'You. Go back to the fields and tell the others I tried to defend the camp. You. Did you hear what I just said?'

I only had one thing on my mind. Rebekah.

Sir Tate grabbed me. 'Boy. I have given you an order. I demand you go and tell them that I have fought off a band of knights. Now, forget about your little whore, and do it.'

I had taken a lot in my life. Growing up in a rough part of town, working just to survive while seeing how the rich and powerful lived, and I had taken it because that's how it had always been. But I had grown, and you did not disrespect the woman I love. I stared at him.

'Go Fuck Yourself.'

Sir Tate grabbed me. I had fought for my country. I had been willing to die for my country. I had killed for my country. And now some rich bully wanted me to treat me like a servant.

He did not move as I leaned back and then lunged forward with every single ounce of force I had left. I headbutted his nose with the precision of an arrow hitting the bullseye. Sir Tate staggered back. There was a moment as he tried to understand what had just happened. Then the pain kicked in. His own blood spurted down his clean armour. He held his hands to his face as I ran to find Rebekah.

She was not among the dead. She was not among the nurses. I picked up my spare arrows. More horses were riding towards the camp.

King Henry arrived with a group of other knights, all covered in mud and blood. He jumped down and cradled a dead boy. The king shouted that this was against all the rules of war. The boy was too young to fight. He couldn't draw a longbow or even pick up a sword. The men who had rode with the King spoke to each other. If the French Knights went back to their camp and reported there were no reserve soldiers, they might attack the English army from the rear. Henry shouted at them that he did not care. The knights drew their swords as the sound of more horses were heard.

The French messenger rode into camp. He looked at the bodies of dead children and said the French knights had acted alone, possibly to find the king and capture him. Henry asked if the French were willing to surrender. The answer was no. The real answer was that no decision had been made. Henry said he had no other choice. He knew there were thousands of French soldier sin reserve. The English were going to kill every wounded knight until the order of surrender was given. The messenger nodded and galloped back through the woods. All the time Sir Michael Tate was telling everyone how he had tried to protect the camp. He eventually pointed at me.

'Arrest that peasant. I found him hiding in the woods like a coward, but I am willing to make him my serf if he agrees that he saw me defending the camp against the French.'
The King and his knights could see I was covered in mud and sweat, just like them. I had blood on my hands, just like them.

'You must be mistaken,' said the King.
Sir Michael Tate moved forward, blood pouring from his nose. 'This working-class scum assaulted me.' He poked a steel gloved finger into my chest. 'I am a knight of the realm.'

'You're a motherless fuck,' I replied. I turned to the King. 'I admit I assaulted this man, after I found him hiding. I am willing to stand trial when I return, but right now I am going back to the battle to stand side by side with my friends.'

The crowd went silent. I had assaulted a knight, and now I was telling the king what to do. I could be killed on the spot.

'We appear to have been here before,' said the King.

'There is a difference, your majesty. Now I am willing to fight for my country, and myself.'
The King climbed back on his horse. 'Do you need a lift?'

Chapter 37

I ran back to the battlefield. The smell of blood and guts fouled the air. I never believed so many men and horses had been undone. The Kings order had been given: Take no prisoners. The English knights were standing back. The English foot soldiers were pushing back. It was the English archers who were ruthless in its command. The working class were saving their country by doing what he had asked. They could still see twenty thousand French soldiers on the horizon. Every dead body gave the archers more weapons and armour to protect themselves when the French decided to attack again. But from where I stood, the French generals seemed unable to move. We had held the line.

   As I walked across the field searching for my friends I found it difficult to look down. There is a smell to death that no one knows unless they have been close to a body that has been wrenched open. Its rather like uncooked meat and vomit. Blood also has its own distinct smell. Thousands of gallons had mixed with the water and mud to turn the ground into a dark red sea of death. As I walked over bodies and screaming horses I saw Rebekah near the line of trees.

   She was tending to a young French knight who had been trampled by a horse. Rebekah had helped him to the side of the trees and was giving him poppy seeds and wine from a pouch. I made my way across the mud and asked if she was OK. She kissed me. The French knight was mumbling.

   'What is he saying?' Rebekah asked me.

I got down and listened. The knight asked me who had been victorious. I looked around at all the bodies covered in dirt and blood and told him no one. I told him I was a physician. I then unclasped his chest plate and handed him his sword. The order had been given for our soldiers to kill all prisoners. I dragged him further into the trees and said he should pretend to be dead until the order had been stopped.

    Rebekah went over to help an old English archer under a tree. He called out that he would stay with the young French man. He was not going to hurt anyone. I took off the knights leg plates. The break on his lower right leg was clean. I helped carry him over to the archer. I cut away the knights' breeches and looked around for something to protect his injury.

    'Here,' said the archer. He handed me his longbow. 'I won't need it where I'm going.'
I tried to refuse but he implored me to use it.

    With his axe I cut the longbow into four pieces. I pushed the bone back. Some of the words the Frenchman used I didn't know, but I could guess what they meant. Even the archer winced. I fixed the pieces of the longbow on either side of the break. I got Rebekah to push them together while I wrapped the twine around and tied it off. We gave the young knight some more poppy seeds, washed down with wine, and went to treat the archer.

    He had only one injury. On the right of his face was a small hole. It had not been done by a crossbow bolt or arrow, nor did it look like any knife injury I had ever seen. The archer explained that a French man come down the field with something that was the height of a longbow, but the thickness and shape of a crossbow. The back was made of wood, and the front was a long grey spout with steel contraptions sticking out of it. He apologised for not being able to find the right words.

'I saw an elephant once. Trying to describe such a beast is almost impossible. It was the same with this weapon.'
I laughed and told him I used to look after an elephant at the Tower. I asked him to continue. He said that the knight stopped and then lit the thing like one of those canon they had at Harfleur. The archer turned, then something hit him in the side of the face. He fell, thinking it was an arrow. Realising it was not; he looked over at his assassin. A horse blocked his view, and when it had passed the knight had gone.

The archer had been in earlier battles, but this was a new pain. It was like his blood had been turned into grains of sand, twisting and spinning inside his head. I looked at the wound. It was deep. Dark blood dripped from his lips.

'What is your name, good sir?'

'Roger Hunt.'

I looked at Roger's skull. There was no exit wound. I had to assume that whatever had been fired from this new weapon was still inside the old man.

'We are going to take you back to a physician's tent Roger, where I can take a closer look.'

Roger was not so sure. 'What unit are you from?'

'The latrine unit. But I am studying to be a physician.'

Roger laughed. 'I've got hair on my balls older than you. Sorry miss.'

Rebekah smiled. 'And like those balls on your wedding night Roger, you will be in very safe hands. Harry knows the King.' This seemed to do the trick. 'Ok, but the young French lad comes back with us. I don't believe in attacking wounded men. Do you think we can manage it.'

The knight would use my longbow as a staff, and the archer could be helped by Rebekah to walk back to camp. As we got ready, I saw the French messenger riding down the middle of the field towards the king's banner. It was now such a quagmire that I was surprised the messenger managed to stay on his horse. Some of our men saw him and stopped killing. The messenger called out until he found the king. He handed over a scroll. It was the official declaration of surrender. Those around the King cheered. At once the English Knights began to shout out that we had won. The battle was finally over. I took the pouch of wine and had a drink. Not so much as a celebration of victory, more because we had survived. I handed the pouch to the French knight and told him the battle was over. He took a drink, then thanked me again. He still wanted to go to the English camp, as the mood in the French camp would be one of defeat. I looked up the field at the French army. They still had thousands of soldiers in reserve but for some reason had given up. I smiled at Rebekah. She smiled back and we hugged. The old archer also seemed to have a smile on his face. He was dead.

French soldiers put down their weapons and started to wade through the field with horses and carts to load up the wounded and dead Knights. Silently, and without being ordered, the English men started to help. It didn't matter if they were French or English, knight or serf, they all weighed the same when they were lifted out from the bloodstained soil. Some had sunk so far down they would never be recovered. This had been a land where no man had been at peace, and the living had sought to wreak hell onto each other. But that time was over. Now the ground was getting ready to help those enter the eternal sleep.

Chapter 38

Move him into the sun—
Gently its touch awoke him once,
At home, whispering of fields half-sown.
Always it woke him, even in France,
Until this morning and this snow.
If anything might rouse him now
The kind old sun will know.
    Wilfred Owen, Futility

I helped move the wounded French knight back to our camp. In another field our dead were being laid out for identification. The bodies of the young boys had been hidden away under a white canvas. Sir Michael Tate had ordered them to be searched, just to make sure they had not stolen anything, but could find no one to do it. When he saw me helping a wounded French knight, he drew his sword and began to shout.

'Help. I demand that someone arrest this traitor. Help.'
I kept walking. This was another kick to his manhood. He ran over to me, sword in one hand.

'How dare you assault me and not obey my command. And now you have the temerity to bring the enemy into my camp. Your punishment will be the loss of your nose.' He stood in front of me. 'You. Yes, I am talking to you.' He tried to stop me. 'Do you want to die, here and now?'

Dr Culpepper came out and helped the French knight into the tent. As I stood in the doorway, Sir Tate pointed his sword at me.

'You are going to tell the King that I tried to protect this camp. If you don't, I will have you put on trial and killed for striking a knight.'

It felt as if this had all happened to me before. But this time I was not going to back down. Assaulting a knight was punishable by death. I was willing to face justice, willing to have a trial, and I was willing to be die, but not from this fucking idiot, not today. I had killed and I had seen thousands of men lying dead in a field turned red with blood. I was prepared to face God and be judged. Sir Michael Tate pressed his sword into my chest.

'Say you saw me trying to protect the camp earlier today, and your future as my serf will be well rewarded.'
I shook my head. 'The past was yours, but the futures mine. I'm not afraid of you anymore.'

Sir Tate threw me into the open ground then swung his sword. He turned it to the side then brought it down, hitting me on the arm with the flat surface.

'This scoundrel attacked me,' Sir Tate told the crowd. 'Because I found him hiding behind a hedge like a tramps turd during the battle.'

'You're a lair,' I called back.
Sir Tate pushed me again, goading me to fight back so he could kill me. He jabbed with his sword. 'You're a coward.'
I parried with my longbow. 'I will stand trial and swear on the Bible I came from the battle and found you hiding.'
I looked into his eyes, and knew Sir Tate wanted to kill me. He turned the sword. Judgement was about to be delivered.

Looking back to that moment, I can honestly say I did not see it coming. Nor did Sir Tate. A shovel hit the side of his arm with such force the vibration created a sound like a bell being struck. Sir Tate dropped to the ground. Every plate of armour seemed to fold and clank as the man lay on his back. Pieshop waited until Sir Tate recovered enough to look up at this new assailant. Pieshop, covered in mud and blood as if borne out of the earth itself, raised the sharpened shovel over the polished breast plate, ready to bring it down on his neck. The crowd around us grew quiet.

'No,' called out Rebekah as she ran towards us. 'This would be wrong. Go for his testicles. There's no chain mail under the crutch.'

Pieshop moved the shovel so that it hung below the waist. Sir Tate begged for mercy. Pieshop got ready.

'Where is my son?'

Sir Tate clasped the palms of his hands together as if in prayer. 'I don't know.'

Pieshop raised the shovel. 'Where is my son?'

The shovel was sharp enough to cut through brick.

'Stop.' King Henry walked forward.

Sir Michael Tate grovelled. 'I want these men arrested. The young one assaulted me, you saw it, and this brute just tried to kill me.'

King Henry, a man who had almost lost a country but instead won a great victory, was not in the mood to hear a long series of confessions. He turned to me. 'Why did you assault your superior?'

I had my answer. 'He has been a bully to all those around him. He has shown no compassion, he has shown no charity, and he has shown no courage. I came back to get more arrows and found him hiding in the bushes. He wanted me to lie and say that he tried to protect the camp. I refused. He then disrespected a nurse. I was raised to be a man, and a gentleman, and an Englishman. I will admit to striking him, but only because I believe he was going to assault me.'

'That doesn't matter. You are still only a serf.' The king turned to Pieshop. 'And why did you assault Sir Michael Tate?'

'Sir Michael Tate's role was to protect the women and children,' Pieshop replied. 'My son was here, and now I cannot find him.'

'He ran away,' the knight called back. 'I demand justice.' The king raised a hand for Sir Tate to be silent. 'These men have done their duty and served their country well. As of this moment, and on this day, I grant them their freedom from any past transgressions.' He looked around at the crowd of men. 'You men, you have all gained your freedom this day. From now on, those who fought on the battlefield with me will be considered my brother, and we shall spend the rest of our lives telling tales to those who will curse that they were not here with us. Rejoice men of England. God has granted us a great victory.' As the men cheered, the king led Pieshop away.

I saw the others. Derryck had a cut on his face, Tony was covered in mud, Icky had bent his battle-axe, Vic had an injury to his arm, Barry's leg was bleeding again, but they were all alive. Nobody could understand the confusion of those last few hours among the mud and blood. We thanked God we had survived the day. It was then that we saw Pieshop as he moved through the crowds. We called out but he did not seem to hear. We followed in silence.

He found him laid out on a white canvas looking up at the gentle sun. There were marks on the palms of his hands. His forehead was congealed with dark red blood that matted his hair. Underneath, his skull had been fractured by a single blow. He must have fallen straight away, as his eyes were open and the blood had dripped down across his forehead. Gently, we moved him onto the back of a cart. He was surprisingly light. Perhaps it is the weight of time that holds us down on this mortal coil. The years toll like passing bells gathering dust until the heart beats no more. His eyes stared at us, although he could not see his father looking down upon him.

The wounded French knight knew a local priest. He pressed his signet ring into some melted wax to use it as a form of credit. We set off to find the church in Saint-Pol-sur-Ternoise just a few miles away.

Vic steered the horse. Pieshop sat next to him. They sat in silence. I realised Pieshop had been wounded on his upper left arm as his sleeve was soaked with his own blood. I sat next to Derryck in the back of the cart. Opposite were Icky and Tony. How strange it was that Pieshop's son, lying in the back of the cart, was the cleanest among us.

As we travelled down half known lanes a few people came out and asked us what had happened. We stayed silent. By the time we reached the small village, the sun was already beginning to slip silently into a grave of grey clouds.

We found the churchyard. It was the sort of place we would only go when we're grey and old. But a child needed to be buried. The priest, fearing he would be robbed, had locked himself in the tower. I showed him the French knight's seal. The priest said the boy would have to be buried in an unmarked grave, name unknown, as someone might dig him up later. We found a spot near the edge of the churchyard that looked out onto some fields.

'He always liked animals,' said Pieshop. 'I think he trusted them more than people. He said they had never let him down. I don't know if he was talking about me or…' He could not finish his words.

We went to dig a small grave. Pieshop stopped us and took the shovel. 'I brought my boy into this world; I'm going to be the one to take him out of it.'

He measured out the grave twice and cut deep into the cold virgin soil once. His wounded arm, with the tattoo of the cross that he had got in Jerusalem, was bleeding heavily. He could barely move the wooden handle to lift out the earth. He stopped. He got down on one knee and rested his good arm on the shovel handle. We knew he was broken. What good is a man if he cannot protect those he loves? No one really knew what to say. It's hard, but it's harder to ignore it. We got our shovels.

It was the smallest grave we had ever dug. We finished as the dusk buried the last drops of light. Pieshop cleaned his sons face with Holy water then wrapped the boy in his tunic, the white cross on his young chest. The father hugged his son for the final time. The ancient Egyptians believed we all die twice; once when we draw our last breath, the next when someone says your name for the very last time. I wanted this boy to be remembered. I wanted people to say his name in a thousand years' from now and remember he sacrificed his today so that those now living could enjoy their tomorrow.

We waited. No one wanted to pour dirt over a dead child. There was only one thing for it. We let the horse go in the field and began to dismantle the wooden cart with our hands. Pulling off the sides and breaking the base, we managed to make a vessel fit for a King. We used the horse rope and our longbow strings to fix the box together, then laid the boy inside the coffin. Once in the ground, we were ready.

Only a father knows how much they have really loved their son, even if they hardly said it. Pieshop looked up as the universe began to reveal itself in the darkening sky.

'Behold, my boy.'

We stepped away to leave Pieshop alone with his memories. At that moment we would have all given to suffer in some way for father his son to have just a few more moments together. Rather than shovel the earth back in, Pieshop took clumps of soil and gently began to place them on the wood, talking under his breath. Eventually there was enough for us to help without disturbing the body. Like sand in an hourglass, the soil did not land where it had been before, but it did not matter.

Pieshop marked the grave with a simple cross made from his Yew longbow. No name, no date of birth, no date of death. Nothing to tell anyone passing that here lay the body of a young boy, all those his hopes and fears cut short by fate.

By the time we walked back to the camp we could see large fires were started. The English had helped carry the dead French up to their camp. The French returned the respect by giving us food and wine. The battle was over. There were no winners, no losers, only those who were dead, and those who had survived.

I went into Dr Culpepper's tent. He was checking on the French knight and was impressed with my basic leg brace. The French knight gave me his father's Templar sword and asked me to write to him when I returned to England. He then gave me food and three jugs of wine. I told Culpepper of the archer with the strange wound that had killed him. No canons had been fired during the battle. Perhaps the injury was caused by the oldest weapon of mankind, a sharpened stick.

I went back to my friends to share the food and wine. They were sitting around a fire. Pieshop, Vic, Derryck, Icky, and Barry all had physical injuries. Vic sat in silence while Tony prepared our food. At some point Pieshop poured some wine into a cup, broke his piece of bread, and went to move. Then he remembered. Slowly, he sat back down. I told the others I was going to give some food to Rebekah.

I found her with the last of the blanket that had been given to her in England. She had been using it as bandages all this time. We found somewhere quiet under the stars. I wrapped her in my cloak and said nothing while she ate. As I went to put my arm around her, I noticed my hand was shaking. I tried to stop it but could not.

'Becky, do you think I am a good man?'

She could not know of what I had seen and done on this day, and I knew I would never tell her everything, but I needed someone to hold me.

'Yes,' she said. It was that simple, and that profound. She didn't explain. I didn't want her to. A woman with the warmest heart I had ever known had looked into my soul and judged me as someone who even with all my faults was good enough to be with her. She hugged me. I put my face into her chest as I did not want her to see me crying. Around us the dead were being moved to their final resting place, waiting for their names to be said for the very last time.

Going back to the camp, we had all in some ways been thrown together by circumstances beyond our control, with some at the top of the hourglass, and others trapped at the bottom. Derryck had sold some gear to buy a French Lute. Vic played a tune. In the darkness Rebekah began to sing. All the soldiers stopped to listen. We had managed to survive a morning where life and death were like grains of sand in the hands of another; and now the remorseful day was over.

PART 5

THE PAST IS ANOTHER COUNTRY

Chapter 39

That was a memorable day to me, for it made great changes in me. But it is the same with any life. Imagine one selected day struck out of it and think how different its course would have been. Pause you who read this and think for a moment of the long chain of iron or gold, of thorns or flowers, that would never have bound you, but for the formation of the first link on one memorable day.
  Charles Dickens, Great Expectations

We woke up just after dawn. The screaming of the horses had gone on throughout the night. A few men were given the task of dispatching them. This included Tony. Arrows were of no use. Men would have to get close enough to push a sharp spike into the horse's heart. They tried to drag the dead horses away by using other horses, but they could not move in the mud. The only other way was for the horses to be cut up where they lay and the carcasses carried to either encampment. The smell of so many of them being cooked over fires meant I would never eat horsemeat again. We wanted to be on the move.

  The French dauphin had signed the surrender agreement. But the French king was not yet aware, and nor were the six thousand French soldiers heading our way. Paris was three hundred miles to the East; Calais was three hundred miles to the West. Henry ordered us to wait together until the rest of the French army arrived and agreed to the surrender. We would spend the next three days helping to bury the French dead.

  As there were so many French wounded and I could speak the language, I was given special dispensation to set up my own infirmary. The French knights wanted to know who had survived or died in the battle. A change of lineage could mean more land and more wealth. For a small fee Vic would go off and make enquiries, Pieshop would go to the stables and make sure their horses had not been rebranded, Tony would obtain wine and cook them a succulent French meal. It was democracy manifest. I would clean the knights of their wounds. Derryck and Icky would clean the men of their armour, weapons, and jewellery, and whenever the knights got a bit too cocky, Barry would strip naked in front of them to have his thigh checked.

On the third day Culpepper took me to one side. He had asked the King to make me an honorary doctor. The King had denied the request. I had not attended university. Culpepper recommended I become an alchemist. I could carry the medical symbol, which gave me the freedom to travel, treat poorer patients, and dispense medicine. He then told me I could stay in St. Albans to finish my apprenticeship. I thanked him and said I would speak to Rebekah first. We stopped as King Henry stood on the top of a cart to call the men over. His tunic, emblazoned with three lions, was covered in dirt and blood. He asked his band of men in the camp to gather around him.

He told us how it had been a long campaign, filled with many hardships, but it was clear from the start that God had blessed us all on this noble undertaking. We had taken part in a great crusade that had seen us travel hundreds of miles away from our homes to fight the enemy. The months of training and the moments of fear had allowed us to form a bond with others, and it had given us friendships that we would carry with us for the rest of our lives. What we few men had done was to save England. Without the courage of your convictions, a devotion to duty, and skill in battle, we could have faced defeat. We had finally done what we had been waiting a thousand years for. On the 25th of October 1415 we had proven to God that England would never be invaded again.

The men around me cheered. The number of English Knights taken by the French, none. The number of English wounded, six hundred. The number of English dead, four hundred. The number of French prisoners taken, three thousand. They had all been released. The number of French wounded and dead, over ten thousand. So many that they were still on the field waiting to be buried three days later.

Now officially part of the physicians unit, I was told I would be one of the last to leave Agincourt. Quite simply, there were those in the infirmary tents who would not survive the journey. Dr Culpepper would make the ultimate decision to use the last of the opium to send the men into an eternal morphine dream. Rebekah would stay. My friends said they would stay as well. Those who did their bit deserved a decent burial. We watched as the men began to leave. It would be another few days before we were ready to go.

It was Rebekah who found him. He was lying in the woods. From a distance it looked as if he had fallen asleep with a smile on his face. It was only when you got closer that you could see it was a contorted grimace. He must have been in pain before he died. Dr Culpepper checked the dead body. He ascertained Sir Michael Tate had of a heart malady. My diagnosis was he had been poisoned, but I said nothing.

Pieshop hadn't said much since the battle. His wound had not healed properly because he insisted on helping to carry and bury the French dead. Derryck said that if Pieshop had killed a knight he would be hung drawn and quartered. You could say it was moral justice, an eye for an eye. Just another grain of blood coloured sand in the hourglass of battle. Who would notice one more dead man in a place that had been filled with ten thousand dead bodies. We took the body out to the fields to bury it.

When we came back we were told to look sharp, we were leaving Agincourt, and going home.

Chapter 40

I've seen things you people wouldn't believe. Attack ships on fire off the shoulder of Orion. I watched C-beams glitter in the dark near the Tannhäuser Gate. All those moments will be lost in time, like... tears in rain.
   Blade Runner.

We packed only what we needed. I took my longbow. I had the Elephant Stone, the Templar sword, and Arthur's amulet. I left the shovel. I didn't want to dig another grave. Everything else would be left to the scavengers waiting in the woods. We loaded the carts in silence. Nobody wants a victory parade through a graveyard. I said goodbye to the French knight with the promise to learn how to use the sword, and he would teach me chess. Many of his comrades were still trying to figure out what tactics went wrong and why we had won. In truth the French had no tactics. They expect us to surrender. When we never, rather than surveying the field to see what would be the best move, they tried to gallop a long distance over deeply ploughed rain-soaked mud. They did not turn around when they came into the killing range of our longbows and deploy their own crossbow units. They should have made the foot soldiers marching straight down the middle of the muddy field into hundreds of fleeing horses turn around and go through the woods to outflank us.

These lack of decision had been so catastrophic, anyone would have beaten the French on that day. Perhaps that is too harsh, on us. If the French had been more respectful of the English lions and remembered that a cornered animal is more dangerous than a subdued one, they might have seen that their vaulting ambition would overleap itself.

As we made our way towards home, I pondered how the English are a strange breed. This island race, so filled with petty squabbles in the streets, pubs, villages and towns, was ready to fight for its history and culture no matter how big and dangerous the foe. In Dunkirk we waited with the Duke of York for the ships to come in. It was Barry Cheeseman who was the first of the gang to go. England was too cold as far as he was concerned. There was a ship he had sailed on before, transporting barrels of cheese that were bound for Cadiz. As he was unable to work due to his injury, we clubbed together and got him a paid passage. We took him to a sailor's tavern for one last drink. Barry sipped on something from the Orient called "Cha", a type of tea which came from dried leaves and looked and tasted like hot horse piss. It would never catch on in England.

Vic Flange then said he wasn't coming back. He was going to travel down to Rome. Apparently, it was the place to be for all aspiring artists in the 14th century. I asked him if we would ever meet again. He said he expected great things from me because I had been a part of something bigger than myself. History had marked me out as someone special.

'There could be another reason why so much has happened to him,' said Derryck. 'He could be…what's the word I'm looking for?…oh yeah, thick. Let's be honest. All these things could have happened to him because he was too stupid to avoid them.' He turned to Vic. 'Won't you get bored travelling around on your own?'

'I'm not,' said Vic. 'I'm going with Nigel Fairservice.' This was the same man who wanted a flying corps in the military, which seemed to consist of muscular men wearing feathers. We all knew what Vic meant. Derryck spoke next.

'To be honest Vic, I'm a bit shocked. I can't believe you think he's better looking than any of us.'
We laughed and joked. It was the first time I had seen Pieshop smile since the battle. Tony went over and kissed Vic on the side of the head. He said he didn't care. Vic was his brother, and whenever he needed help, Tony would be beside him. We all agreed. Vic hugged us all. He left singing a song,

'And when they ask us how dangerous it was,
We'll never tell them, no, we'll never tell them:
We spent our pay in some cafe,
And fought wild women night and day,
Twas the cushiest job we ever had.'

The rest of the men in the tavern joined in with the second chorus as Vic opened the tavern door. Outside, coffins returning home were being carried down to the sea and take their last journey across the water.

The next morning, we got on the ship. Our journey across the channel was rougher than before. I stood with Rebekah on the deck as the white cliffs of Dover came into view. From Canterbury Cathedral you took the pilgrims road to London. Perhaps it didn't matter. I would be moving with Becky to St. Albans. Minstrels and poets had courtly love; but for me, the woman I cuddled in bed with every night was all I needed. And you can keep all your fancy statues and paintings. It made me happy just to squeeze her bum every day.

Before we docked, our Italian cook, Rigalaroni Tony, was the next to go. The captain told him that a ship, *The Holigost*, was to be refitted with cannons. A job was going in the kitchens. Tony had found that being at sea made his St. Vitus dance invisible, and his swearing was an added bonus when it came to being a chef. He told us he would be staying on board and sailing down to Portsmouth.

It was November when we landed. Three months since I had last stepped on English soil. My feet felt like they were walking on Jerusalem. We went with Dr Culpepper and the King to Canterbury cathedral to pray and give thanks to our victory. We stayed in Kent for two weeks while the knights waited to be collected and taken back to their shires. Pieshop built crutches, Icky supplied patients with ale or hemp cakes. Derryck, along with Ophelia McKracken who had come to meet him, supplied them with women. We were not really soldiers anymore. It was time for us to move on.

We moved through the villages of England. Stopping near an old Ale house, Icky fell in love with a widow called Stella. I gave Icky the hop seeds I had brought back from France and explained how they used it to make a special type of beer. The hops were easy to grow, the fermenting process was cheaper, and the stuff tasted better than most ales. Stella was worried as hops were labelled as a "pernicious weed" and had been banned in England. This was manna from Heaven for Icky, who believed that the secret ingredient for anything enjoyable was crime. And so, one more of the band of bastards left the group.

Dr Culpepper said he was going straight on to St. Albans. We stopped in a tavern near Southwark Cathedral. Now it was time for Derryck to say goodbye. He was going to offload all the armour before Christmas. With the money he and Ophelia McKracken had saved, they were going to buy a house in Shepherd Market, near Mayfair, and set it up as an exclusive brothel. He had found out that Knights, Dukes, and politicians all wanted to be spanked by scantily clad wenches; and they were willing to pay well for it. He took me to one side and said that if money was ever tight to come and see him. He could get Rebecca a job no problem. I thanked him and we hugged. Derryck may have been a short, arsed cockney, but when it came to standing by your friends and fighting for what you believe in, he was a giant. Once we offloaded the hooky gear, he gave us the horse and cart as a wedding gift.

Me, Pieshop and Rebekah crossed London Bridge. We must have looked quite a sight. I had my longbow and still wore my tunic. I knew that once I took it off, the war was officially over. Once we reached the other side of the river our duties to the crown would be complete. Everyone man must go back to their shires at some point in their lives. Some come back to a hero's return, while others would creep back, silent, to still village wells, and up half-known roads, to realise just how much of their past had changed. I wondered how Pieshop would be greeted. His wife would be waiting, lining up the cutlery and pulling out the cork. She may even see him from a distance as he walked over England's green and pleasant land. Her countenance would change as she realised her son, her lamb of God, had been sacrificed to save this country. Would she ask her husband why it was that their son that had died while others had lived?

We said our goodbyes outside All Hallows. I still had to find out more about my father, and his death. Pieshop was not my dad, but he had been there during my transition from a boy to a man. He had tried to steer me down the right path. He had protected me and then taught me how to protect others. I said that although I had lost one father as a boy, I found a new one who had made me a man. He hugged me and said that I should always aim to be the best I could be, and to fear God. He kissed Rebekah and said he expected to see her again as well. He walked off, heading north towards the Essex Road.

We travelled east into Whitechapel. I stored the horse and cart in stables just off Bucks Row. I had my longbow, my sword, and my pack filled with various items I had got in France. Rebekah had her backpack filled with jars of medicine. She was amazed at how many streets and people there were in

London. The local market, crowded with traders and shoppers, were all speaking in an accent that was called "Cockney". I had never noticed it until Rebekah pointed out that since we had got to London, I had started speaking the same dialect. After a few more streets I started to meet friends, acquaintances, and stall holders. They all wanted to shake my hand and welcome me back home.

My mum cried when she saw me. The months had felt like years for her. I never realised just how much time she had spent protecting me when I was just a boy until I saw her looking so weak. While I had been away, I had grown in stature. She kept telling me how much I now looked like my father, then complained I had cut my hair too short. I thought of telling her what Pieshop told me about my father but decided not to. That was the past. I introduced her to my future, Rebekah. They chatted for what seemed like forever (well, it was more my mother trying to get as much information as possible about Rebekah and us). After Rebekah had answered a series of lengthy questions about our relationship, I told my mum I was going to be an apprentices physician in St. Albans. It wasn't quite true, but it sounded good.

I gave my younger brother a French coin and told him he could have my bed. I gave my older brother the Elephant Stone and told him he could have my job at the tower.

People from the manor came in to see me. Everyone wanted to take me for a drink. Becky said we should, so we all went to our local, *The Blind Beggar,* with the prospect of getting absolutely hammered. The word over London was that the English had won a famous battle against all the odds. Was it true the French army numbered over fifty thousand men? Was it true the English archers fired so many arrows they darkened the sky? Did Henry order three thousand prisoners to be killed. Did the French sneak behind the lines and kill all the English women and children? My mum told them that the last question was rubbish, as my girlfriend Rebekah had been there (for the rest of her life she always called her Rebekah, never Becky or Becks).

I think my mum was more proud of me having a bird and settling down than she was of me having a dust up. My uncle Albie put his arm around my shoulder and whispered to me, well done. I told him I was just doing my duty during the battle. He looked at my girlfriend and said, yeah, and that as well. More questions. Already there were people who didn't want the truth about war. They wanted the story, the drama, the highlights.

I told them about the people I had met, the training, knocking an arrow out of a bullseye, how we got lost on our first day abroad, got into a fight with a goat that only understood French, and how one of my friends was captured and had his fingers cut off. I showed them how at the battle our archers raised their two fingers to the French army to prove they were ready to fight. This became the cockney salute.

Everyone wanted to know the big drama, the great moments, the stuff you put on a tapestry screen. But for me, it was all those times with my friends when we were just enjoying each other's company and having a laugh that I now recall most fondly. I joked with the people in the pub, but I was already beginning to miss being with my brothers in arms. The only good thing was putting my arm around Becky's waist as I chatted to friends at the bar.

The next morning, I went to see Rodney's mum. I told her he had died during the siege of Harfleur, saving the lives of his fellow Englishmen. I was not there, as I was not good enough to be a soldier like him, but I know he received a Christian burial, and even the King bowed his head. Then I went to the tower to see my old master, Sir Jeffrey Bernard, and told him that I was going to be an apprentice alchemist with Dr Culpepper. We celebrated with a bottle of wine. As we spoke there was shouting and cheering from outside.

We walked through the courtyard. A strange weapon was on display. It was called a Musket, and it was going to change the history of warfare. Working on the same principle as the canon, it could be used by anyone with the minimum of practice. Even a child would now have the power to kill. My old master shook his head. He believed in the sword was an elegant weapon for a more civilised age.

On our own horse and cart, we left London. We stopped at Boreham Wood to see Rebekah's relatives. I am not saying the place is rough, but if Becky had not said who were family were, the kids would have stolen the wheels off our cart. Then we went to Shenley to see her mother. She handed Becky the gold that Arthur had given her to look after. Reverend Peters said that with the permission of the Hawksmoor family we could be married in St. Botolph's church on Christmas Day. We moved on. At the setting of the sun, we saw the tower of St. Albans cathedral in the distance. A new journey for us was about to begin.

Chapter 41

And in the end, the love you take is equal to the love you make.
   The Beatles.

Lord Farquar's gold was enough to buy a smallholding in what was to later become King Harry Lane. I continued to work as an apprentice with Dr Culpepper. I also improved my education by teaching the boys' archery and swordsmanship at St. Albans school. Being an alchemist made me famous in my later years. Looking back, the work and the money were not really important. Spending time with Becky, listening to her talk about her day, massaging her shoulders when she was tired, cooking her a nice meal, fixing the furniture as soon as she asked, telling her how beautiful she looked in a new dress she had made, they were the important things.

We had four children, although one died while young. Then we had fifteen grandchildren. One of the girls, Rebecca, was the one most like Rebekah, and she is now my nurse.

I did meet with some of the others again. Derryck had become rich after opening a brothel called *The Legionnaires Club*. Ophelia became pregnant, and they had a little boy. Derryck's biggest dream was that his offspring would never do a hard day's work in their lives. Barry made his way to England. Derryck got him a job as a carriage driver even though he knew nothing about horses. Barry earned extra money in Derryck's brothel from politicians and noblemen who paid to watch Barry have sex (with women, not horses).

Tony spent a few years in the Navy before opening a tavern in London where people could also dance. Vic and Nigel Fairservice (who left the army under mysterious circumstances) travelled to the greatest cities in the four known corners of the earth: Cairo, Beijing, Moscow, Norwich. For a while they joined Reginald Kincaid and his band of travelling troubadours, until Kincaid was arrested for various offences, including lascivious drunkenness, lecherous behavior in a nunnery, fouling the air during a school nativity play, and attempted buggery of a root vegetable. He was banned from ever performing at children's parties again. Later he was made Lord Mayor of Watford. Vic Flange spent a happy retirement with Nigel singing songs in Glastonbury. His nephew later went to America and founded the town of Gobbler's Knob in Punxsutawney.

Icky remained with Stella. Although she was a lot older than him, Icky said it didn't matter; he loved every single hair on that woman's chin. We helped set up a small brewery in Kent using the hops from France. My younger brother and his family would sometimes leave the east end in the summer and go down to help pick the harvest.

I was involved in the two battles of St. Albans. The first in 1455, the second 1461, part of what they now call "The Wars of the Roses". Being too old to fight, but I noticed that the same rules still applied from when I was a boy. The generals make all the promises and plans. The young men do all the fighting and dying.

My personal plan was to live for three score years and ten and then leave this mortal coil before I had to ask that question that all old men dread, "Who am I?". Better God take me in my sleep than let me wake up and not know what my own name is. It may sound cruel, but I wanted to go first.

Although I never said it enough and I could be a bit of a lazy bastard when we were older, I probably loved her more than she loved me. But it was Rebekah God wanted to meet first. After she had gone, I finally realized that it wasn't God or the universe that had been watching me, it was her. Becky was the one who had continued to love me on those Farty Sunday mornings when I couldn't be bothered to dress properly, when I would sit in moody silence, and when my stomach was bigger than our daughters' pregnant belly. I did not realize how important she was until she had gone.

Now I am looked after by my grandchildren and great grandchildren. But not a day goes by without me thinking of the first time I saw Becky when I was just a boy. The way her eyes shone like the stars, and when she smiled it was the closest thing to heaven I have ever known. Sometimes I think that God sent me an angel because he wanted me to make something of myself. Not Agincourt, but my life in total. And the question I asked her on that day still haunts me: Have I been a good man? My answer is that if Becky found it in her heart to love me, then I must have been. It also means that if I was to die tonight, hers is the first face I would see. That's the best reason I can think of not to fear death.

Chapter 42

I learned that one can never go back, that one should not ever try to go back - that the essence of life is going forward. Life is really a one-way street, isn't it?
   Agatha Christie

London 1501.

That's it. That's the end of my account. I wait for the Tudor Dynasty to let me go. I may be old, but I still have things to do. I want to watch the birds in my garden. I look around the room. The tapestry of the three lions is fraying at the edges. I know the feeling. I cannot say any more about the Battle of Agincourt. I cannot recall everything that the King said or did during the campaign. When it comes to the past, sometimes it's just as horrible to forget as it is to remember. Sometimes I even dream of things that I know never happened.

   My final thought is that the men with me on that day all those years ago wanted England to remain English, and to preserve the things that were important to them, honor, family, loyalty, and pride in their culture. Catherine of Aragon asks a question.

   'Do you think the Battle of Agincourt was the most important thing in the last hundred years?'
I shake my head. 'The printing press changed everything. Before 1400 we were in darkness. The page gave us light.'

   One more question. It comes from the boy Henry.
   'How did you get so old?'
   'Fear God,' I reply. 'And time. Time that passes like sand in an hourglass.

Perhaps the boy prince thinks that my story could also be his, if he was to ever be Henry the Eighth. What does the future hold for him at this moment? Nothing but a life of comfortable drudgery, spending the sunset of his years telling tales of drunkenness and cruelty. Unless of course, fate takes a hand, his older brother dies and he becomes King. He will need to be quick if his brother is to be married to Katherine of Aragon within the year. Spanish women are notoriously fertile, and hairy. I smile at the Spanish maid again. Her eyebrows could eat a lettuce leaf.

And so, I bid you farewell and adieu Spanish ladies. I tip my hat to the new constitution, take a bow to the new revolution and stop in front of the young boy. He speaks again.

'What you have said, was it all true?'

I'm beginning to like this kid. From my cloak I take out a small ivory clasp.

Sir Andrew Marl decides the epilogue should belong to him.

'My honorable guests. To ask, what is truth, is the same as asking, what is man?' Marl struts across the stage, stopping in front of the Spanish contingency. 'England needs to have heroes, although I would suggest they do not have to win wars to gain that status. Christopher Columbus did not have to kill anyone to discover the Americas.'

I smile. He should never have gotten off the boat, I say to myself. Even I know that thousands of Natives have been killed in the last few years. The black Spaniard looks over at me. But Marl continues with his philosophy of killing with kindness.

'Perhaps Columbus made his discovery by pure chance,' he tells the audience. 'And Henry won the battle of Agincourt by pure luck. I believe we should write our heroes the way they should be read by future generations.'

It was a not-so-subtle way of telling me my story was not going to be part of the history of England.

The men carry me out of the room in a sedan chair. We go down the spiral stone steps. In the darkness it is difficult to maneuver. Sir

Marl is behind us, carrying the manuscripts. Once in the courtyard I ask to be left near the cages. The men go off to get my carriage ready. Sir Andrew Marl waits until we are alone.

The elephant cage is empty. The leg chain is still there, as well as the sand, and a smooth line in the flagstones where the captured creature did the same monotonous walk every day of its life. Perhaps that is the best summarization of history I can offer. Time is an elephant. You can be at the good end, feeding it, controlling it, knowing you can cut off the tusks whenever you want. Or you could be at the other end, keeping your head down, spending every day trying to avoid getting covered in shit and hit by a massive nob. For a few, a happy few, fate will smile on them, and they will get the chance to be like Hanibal and sit on the top of the world to see history as it happens. But even an elephant must one day go to the graveyard. I look over at the other cages. The lions are sleeping. Marl stays at my side.

'You failed to mention your other friends, and all the other men you have killed.' He looks through the cages towards the river Thames. 'You see, I have gone through the muster roll of Henry the Fifth. I know the real name of this Pieshop, and his family. I have also checked on the unsolved deaths of merchants in London. My father was murdered in 1435, on the day I was born. The other merchants had an enquiry to find the killer, but nothing came of it. The King does not know any of this yet. He wouldn't want you to be arrested at the tower. I will come to St. Albans. You will not survive one night in jail.'

From my pocket I took out a gold coin and handed it to him. He bit it.

'You would need at least thirty of these for me not to kill you and put your family in prison.'

I am a hundred years old. Death would be peace from aching bones. It's only my family I care for now. I take out three pieces of paper. 'Here is a written confession that I poisoned Sir Michael Tate. You can arrest me, cancel my words, erase me from history, so be it. But I have spoken the truth, and no matter how much you try to hide it, no matter how much you fear it, the truth will always be there, waiting to be unearthed like bones in a ploughed field.'

Marl shook his head. 'I didn't really care about Sir Michael Tate. But the confession will be enough to seize your goods and send your family back to the gutter where they belong.'

I make a verbal parry. 'I have also written down the truth of how your father killed mine.'

Marl shakes his head again. 'It might as well be fiction. No one will read it anyway.'

My last literary chance was a bullseye. I handed him the last page. He glanced at the printed words.

As payment, the monks at All Hallows church taught me how to read and write. They marked me out as someone with high intelligence. I was allowed to study inside churches while my father risked his life repairing the roofs. My knowledge of the Bible and Latin helped my father get work on a lot of great houses. Then in 1413 we arrived the Tower of London to repair part of the roof.

The next thing he heard was the sound of the cage door being locked.

'I too have a confession to make,' I tell Marl. 'You see, I have access to a printing press in St. Albans. When I received your letter to come here, I knew I was walking into a trap. I gave my account to my children for them to print my own book. Of course, some things I have left out, such as the poison on the gold coin.'

Sir Marl stares at me. 'Who are you?'

He begins to cough as the poison reaches his lungs. He lets go of the papers and clutches his chest. Soon the poison will grip his heart. The pieces of paper blow into the river and disappear.

I look across the courtyard. One of the guards is running towards us. Lord Marl falls to the flat stone as he calls to the guard. The die is cast. I look up at the tower. The boy prince is peeping from the artillery room window. Behind me is the sound of a beast finally stirring. A lion comes out of the shadows, ready to roar again.

References

There are plenty of real historical books on Agincourt, giving facts and details of what powerful men said and did and. This is not one of those books. These are just half arsed dreams that swirl around in my ADHD mind bucket. My references come from various moments and phrases that influenced me in writing the novel.

Chapter 1
About teatime. Monty Python, the Life of Brian.
You want to know what happened - Taken from the documentary series The World at War. The comment comes from Siegmund Weltlinger, an elderly gentleman speaking about Crystal Night in 1938, as he watched synagogues being vandalized and Jews being attacked. I did wonder if it was right to start what is essentially a comedic story with such a terrible incident. But The World at War shaped my understanding of history and is still one of the best documentary series ever made.
I have been here before. J.B. Priestley.
Rantallion – The flesh of an old man's scrotum which hangs down further than his flaccid penis.

Chapter 2
Jeffrey Bernard – Soho theatre critic and proverbial drunk.
Bottle of Chianti – Silence of the Lambs.
Battle of Shrewsbury - 21st July 1403.

Chapter 3
Edwin Farriner – believed to have owned the baker shop which started the great fire of London.

Gone a bit flash - From the video of A solid Bond in Your Heart, by the Style Council.
Cunning Plan. Blackadder.

Chapter 4.
Speaking metaphorically – Ripping Yarns, The Curse of the Claw.
Pieshop – Blackadder, A Christmas Carol. "If Tiny Tim gets any bigger, he will be the size of a pie shop."
Derryck Hollins – Hollins was Del Boys mum's maiden name. Only Fools & Horses.
Vic Flange - Played by Sid James in Carry on Abroad.
I'm just a poor boy – Queen, Bohemian Rhapsody.

Chapter 5
Rambling Sid Rumpole – A mixture of Round the Horne (Rumpo) and Rumpole of the Bailey..
It saves time – fairly sure it was a line from the TV series Minder.
Far Diddly Farquar – Adam Ant. Prince Charming.
Ye Olde Fighting Cocks – pub in St. Albans.

Chapter 6.
St. Albans school – Among the alumni is Professor Stephen Hawkins.
Thank God I was a man – Naked Gun.
Andrei Rublev – film by Andre Tarkovsky about a medieval painter.

Chapter 7.
Don't let the bastards grind you down – Porridge.
The Five D's – Dodgeball.
The secret ingredient is crime – Super Hans, Peep Show.

Soup/fork - He's like a man with a fork, in a world of soup – Noel Gallagher.

Chapter 8.
Reginald Kincaid – from the book Holidays in the Sun
He could have been a contender – On the Waterfront.
World of shit – Full metal jacket.
Band of Bastards – Band of Brothers

Chapter 9.
Pride of Life – medieval morality play.
Picture of Man and Two Dogs – Goodfellas. The painting on the wall that looks like someone we know.

Chapter 10
Profound – Sean Connery on learning to read.
Stories, the ones that really mattered – Lord of the Rings
Rise – Pil ltd.
Grabalocker fishwife – The Beatles, I am the Walrus
Scum and villainy – Star Wars (the good ones)
Work together – Gladiator

Chapter 11
Shepherd's spy – The Goons
Village of Chillingbourne – A Canterbury Tale (film by Powell & Pressburger)
The way you wear that dress – Shake Rattle and Roll (Big Joe Turner version)
Lovely Pear – Carry on Doctor
Sweet child of mine – Guns and Roses
Sumer is Icumen in – The Wicker Man
My life's a funny thing – David Bowie, Young Americans

Chapter 12
Spartacus – Stanley Kubrick

Chapter 13
To die for one's country – Wilfred Owen. Dule Et Decorum Est.
Come with me if you want to live – Terminator II
She looked at me with those big brown eyes – Bachman Turner overdrive, You aint seen nothing yet.
Ronnie reality – Red Dwarf

Chapter 14
Best bucket I've had in ages – Ricky Gervais.
Halliwell Manuscript – medieval Poem believed to be the origins of Freemasonry.
Bishop of Bath and wells – Blackadder II
That it should come to this – Lord of the Rings.
What if he just senses it? – Our Day Out, the scene in the zoo, by Willy Russell.
Everybody takes a beating – Goodfellas.

Chapter 15
Comes in colours – The Rolling Stones, She's a Rainbow.
Just a flesh wound – National Lampoons European vacation. Comment made after Eric Idle gets run over.
Brace yourselves – Only Fools and Horses. If you know the episode, you know.
I'm Spartacus – Spartacus
So is my dad – I'm Brian and so is my wife, Life of Brian.

Chapter 16.
Collect your fags – The Jam, Eton Rifles.

Hourglass in a bucket - We start off Man himself. This is classical physics, which is the Greek/Roman Man and how he sees the world.

He is standing by the shore at midday. This is the Renaissance. The man believes the tide is worked by the moon, which is Newtonian physics and the laws of gravity, he just doesn't know it yet.

The arm swinging is Einstein's first theory of relativity, with energy being used to swing the bucket from a singular point on earth.

The rope is string theory.

The bucket is Einsteins second theory of relativity, E+MC2.

The water in the bucket is a link to Stephen Hawkings theory that the universe consists of four dimensions: length, width, height, and time (the bucket spinning through space). But Hawkings believed there was a fifth dimension, the paradox of a parallel universe (the hourglass) in which atoms are constantly shifting. This can be explained by the man swinging a bucket half filled with water, Inside the water is an hourglass, spinning at a different rate than the man's arm. The sand inside the hourglass travels through its smallest point (a black hole) to the other side, then travels back again. No grain of sand ever lands at the same point in space and time, but the same grains of sand are trapped inside the hourglass, much like the planets in space. This leaves us with a possible theory of being able to travel through time and space. Or it could be me talking bollocks.

Lust of the eye – comment made by historian Stephen Ambrose in The World at War.

Great crusade for which we have striven – Speech by Dwight Eisenhower before D Day.

Adds a bit of spice – Withnail and I.

Something to hold on to – Blackadder -Lord Flashheart.

Let him plead -Withnail & I

Chapter 17.
Decameron. 14th Century book by Giovanni Boccaccio.

Chapter 18.
We'll start the war from here – Teddy Roosevelt Jnr on D Day when his ship missed its landing point.
Never get out of the boat – Apocalypse Now.
Derrick Dubois – Only Fools and Horse.
Harry Le Roy – For the life of me I can't remember where I saw the name, probably from some amateur hack.
Booker Newberry III – soul singer.
On the line to dry – The Jam, Town called Malice.
Stay on the path – An American Werewolf in London.

Chapter 19.
Touching cloth – colloquial term for a turd peeking out of the cornhole like a turtles head and nudging on the underpants.
Finest wine known to humanity – Withnail & I
Giddy as a schoolboy – Scrooge, A Christmas Carol.
Keep the change ya filthy animal – Home Alone
It's the buzz – Sexy Beast.

Chapter 20.
Hello honky tonks – Dick Emery
Chattes Fleuries – Flowery Twats – Fawlty Towers would have an anagram on their hotel sign at the start of every episode.
There's a place in Eastbourne – The major in Fawlty Towers.
Queen of the Harpies – Who's Afraid of Virginia Woolf.
Ooh Arthur – On the Buses (I have only ever seen the films, made in Borehamwood).
You're a wizard Harry – Harry Potter (from the film. I don't know if its in the book).

Chapter 21.
I maybe a liar, but I'm an honest one – Frederico Fellini, Italian film director.

Chapter 22
Likes going out and a kicking the balls – should be "Lights going out and a kick in the balls" – The Jam, That's Entertainment. My mishearing it in my youth was due to having a record player that looked like a briefcase and only had one built in speaker.
Smell of elderberries – Monty Python and the Holy Grail
I have become death, the destroyer of worlds – Oppenheimer after the bomb was dropped.

Chapter 23
Allow me to retort – Pulp Fiction
Might Just as well been Closed – Procol Harum
Stared at the sun – Futility, Wilfred Owen.

Chapter 24
Nigel Fairservice – Frasier, Radio Ham, part played by food critic Gill Chesterton.
Bucket and a half – Phoenix Nights
Minkey – Peter sellers, The Pink Panther.

Chapter 25.
The air hangs heavy like a sullen wine – The Smiths, Rusholme Ruffians.

Chapter 26.
Jack Cohen – Founder of Tesco
Down through the heavens – The Stone Roses, Elephant Stone.

Chapter 27.
La Chatte Pourrie – The Rotten Fanny.
Picture yourself on a boat on a river – The Beatles, Lucy in the sky with diamonds.
We are all one- Bill Hicks, one of the world greatest comedians.
Life is brief – from Ikiru, directed by Akira Kurosawa, 1952.
Einar the Viking warrior – I pictured the music from the film The Vikings, 1958, starring Kirk Douglass.

Chapter 28
Beauty will save the world – Fyodor Dostoevsky.

Chapter 29
They would say that, wouldn't they – Mandy Rice Davies. Who Killed Stephen Ward.
Fighting on the beaches – Winston Churchill
End of the beginning – Winston Churchill

Chapter 30
A boat floats and a stone sinks – The Rings of Power. An abomination.

Chapter 31
A cold coming we had of it – T. S. Elliot, Journey of the Magi.
Wound my heart with a monotonous languor – code used on French radio in 1944 to alert the resistance that D Day had started.
Not down on any map, true places never are – Herman Melville, Moby Dick.

Chapter 32
Looked upon the works of a mighty empire, and despaired – Shelley, from the poem Ozymandias.
Son and heir of nothing in particular – The Smiths, How soon is now?
Is it safe? – The Marathon Man (the dentist scene).
Greatest shot I've ever seen – The Magnificent Seven.
C'est un piège – It's a trap – Star Wars (film).
Its in the trees, its coming – Night of the Demon.
Splinter of the Minds Eye- Star Wars (part of the book series)
We who are about to die – oath of the gladiator.

Chapter 33
Do you know how to spell bugger off? – Local hero.
Think of where you want to be – Gladiator (the film)
And me – scene from Dad's Army where the old men all agree to fight the Nazis (even to the death). I think it was the last ever episode and was quite moving.

Chapter 34
Two riders were approaching – All Along the Watchtower (Jimi Hendrix version)
The battle - Part of this story comes from the account of Jean le Fèvre de Saint-Remy. He is known as the authority Toison d'or (Golden Fleece) because he served as the King of Arms to the Order of the Golden Fleece.

Chapter 35
Encore une fois – Sash. 90's dance song.

Chapter 36
Go fuck yourself – Spider in Goodfellas.

Chapter 37
Had been undone – T.S. Eliot, The Waste Land.
Roger Hunt – From the reports at Agincourt, he is believed to be the first English soldier to have ever been killed by a rifle.

Chapter 38
The past was yours but the futures mine – The Stone Roses, She Bangs the Drums.
Saint-Pol-sur-Ternoise – churchyard where the unknown soldier from WW1 was dug up and taken to Westminster Abbey.
Grey and old – Robbie Williams, Angels.
It's hard, but even harder to ignore it – Cat stevens, Father and Son.
Fires were started – Humphrey Jennings, Fires Were Started, documentary for WW2
The Remorseful Day – A. E. Housman, How Clear, How Lovely Bright.

Chapter 39
Succulent French meal – succulent Chinese meal, democracy manifest - the arrest of Jack Karlson from a Chinese restaurant. He was innocent.
A long campaign – Band of Brothers, scene where Major Winters watches a German General give a speech to his men about the bonds of comradeship.
A noble undertaking – Eisenhower's speech to American servicemen on the eve of D Day.

Chapter 40
First of the gang to go – Morrisey, First of the Gang to Die.
And When They Ask Us- from the film version of Oh what a Lovely War, by Jerome Kern & Me Rourke.

The Holigost – The Holy Ghost, medieval warship, which later sank in 1422 in the river Hamble, Hampshire.
Creep back, silent, to still village wells, Up half-known roads - The Send-Off, by Wilfred Owen
Bucks Row – linked to Jack the Ripper and the murder of Polly Nichols.
Blind Beggar pub – where Ronnie Kray shot George Cornell.
Elegant weapon for a more civilized age – Obi Wan Kenobi, Star Wars, filmed in Borehamwood.

Chapter 41
Gobblers Knob – Groundhog Day
Who is it that can tell me who I am? – Shakespear, King Lear.
Closest thing to Heaven – song by The Kane Gang.

Chapter 42
Drunkenness and Cruelty – The Kinks, Sunny Afternoon.
Farewell and adieu Spanish ladies - Jaws.
Tip my hat to the new constitution – The Who, Won't get fooled again.

Printed in Great Britain
by Amazon